COLLECTED POEMS

1967-2006

BY ANNE BERESFORD:

Walking without Moving (Turret Books 1967)
The Lair (Rapp And Whiting 1968)
Footsteps on Snow (Agenda Editions 1972)
The Curving Shore (Agenda Editions 1975)
Songs a Thracian Taught Me (Marion Boyars 1980)
Songs from God's Country (Yoxford Publications 1980)
The Sele of the Morning (Agenda Editions 1988)
Snapshots from an Album 1884-1895 (Katabasis 1992)
Charm with Stones / Zauberspruch mit Steinen
(Bilingual Text: Shriftenreihe Lyrik im Hölderlin Turm, Tübingen 1993)
Landscape with Figures (Agenda Editions 1994)
Selected and New Poems (Agenda Editions & Bellew Publishing 1997)
No Place for Cowards (Katabasis 1998)
Hearing Things (Katabasis 2002)
Poems by Anne Beresford and Angela Brown (limited edition, the One time Press 2005)

TRANSLATION
Alexandros, Selected Poems by Vera Lungu, (Agenda Editions 1975**)**

Collected Poems

1967-2006

Anne Beresford

KATABASIS

First published in September 2006 by KATABASIS
10 St Martin's Close, London NW1 0HR (0207 485 3830)
katabasis@katabasis.co.uk
http://www.katabasis.co.uk
Copyright © Anne Beresford 2006
Printed and bound by CLE Print,
Media House, Burrel Road, St Ives,
Huntingdon PE27 3LE (01480 465233)
Cover illustration: Claire Hamburger
Typeset in-house mainly in 12 point Garamond.

Trade Distribution: Central Books
99 Wallis Road
London E9 5LN
(020 8986 4854)
ISBN: 0904872 42 4

British Library Cataloguing in Publication Data:
A catalogue record for this book is available
from the British Library.

Katabasis is grateful for the support of the Arts Council of England.

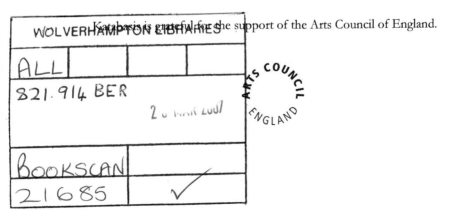

Contents

At the Present Moment

the buds are not certain
whether they will flower
the clouds may be blown away
the sea calm now
may suddenly rise in tidal waves
and flood the town

sirens screaming in Camberwell
screaming in Fifth Avenue
screaming in Menton
that car may be the next
to crash
that house the next
to burn now
for someone

when you are there
it is now
time is the calling of pheasants
on a clear evening
the brown earth
of the ploughed field
the tree's roots spreading
over and under the brown earth
so we stood uncertain
near to being children

now there are buses
the room
the twigs scratching
at the window
like chalk on a blackboard
the birds chirruping

now before dark
a stranger alone
in a strange house
groping fingers
to find the light
hair touching the floor
uncertain of dust
and silence
now being now

Waiting

the cicada's cry is not heard
mountain caves have no hermits now
through avenues of plane trees
I shivered
and the house stood above
the sea

they stopped me then
you are the one
they said
you have been ordered to collect
the dead

in the town hall
with its polished floors
and curving stair
they asked me:
where is your passport
where are your papers?
we employ clowns for jobs like this
it's more amusing

but you must wait while we enquire
why you are here
suddenly the sun has opened up the valley
and the house can watch
the twisting road
waiting for me to come
in this corridor I sit on a hard chair
and in my head I feel
the heat

♪

Inversion

the cat carries my children in her mouth
and teaches them
to catch mice

squirrels hang by their tails from branches
eating bananas

rats pick apples in our orchard
to store in the cellar
later they will put down poison
to keep us out

in the kitchen strangers sit drinking water
and watching the egg-timer
two of my four arms are amputated
so now I am human

and filled with remembrance of syringas
you stand by the canal
forgotten fears protected by sunglasses

the inquisition of graves has revealed bones
and the narrowness
of identification

♪

Blackbird

singing
a blackbird
in the rhododendrons
wildly
but hidden by red blossom
for the child
watching rustling leaves
from the window
it is better
than a nightingale
there is a smell
of damp earth
and country drains
this morning
in the spinney
an egg speckled
fragile unbroken
and primroses
growing in moss
the child listens
and understands
as in childhood

Saturday in New York

on Saturday on Saturday
people look at elephants in
the children's zoo
they look at tigers
and at yaks
they eat peanuts and candy

poverty is personal
said the four cripples

don't feed or annoy
the animals
don't put garbage in the street
the sky is the same colour
even in Harlem

slums have gotten worse
said the democratic candidate

hurry across Central Park
hurry down Broadway
don't look at your neighbour
he may be a Puerto Rican
he may want to rape you
don't feed or annoy
the communists

the wind blows ice from the sea
said the old lady in the wheel chair

Tête à Tête

we talk
I like to look at you
we are not improper
love of course wouldn't do
we have been brought up carefully
but I would rather you ate me
than sit here quietly discussing art

♪

Prison without Bars

the days are real
must be
the milkman calls each morning
the children leave for school
as usual
the newspapers report on crime
on accidents on war
it happens

have you a medal for killing?
do you use the latest deodorant?
are you a blood donor?
whose side are you on anyway?

the ashes are raked from the fire
the rooms are empty
someone has stepped
out of line
someone is trying to get loose

they will get you
whisper the neighbours
it's not allowed to walk
without crutches
the rag and bone man rings a bell:
bring out your dead
bring out your dead

♪

The Windrush

outside in cold mist
the willows drew their swords
and fought
while the river rushed past
whispering over the stones

I will kill the woman
I will take the man
the river hissed
but whatever they drop
into my water
I will carry it away

swiftly at nightfall
past the willow trees
I will drown their cries

and the swans
will bow their heads
and with their necks long
fly
across the low flat fields

The Fates

this living
which I can't do
adds up to something
always preying
on someone
in some tree
doing the right thing
at the right moment
the horse cropping grass
even when it rains

you busy
passing your eye
from one to the other
or shaking dice
playing snakes and ladders
hands trembling
you could be older

when you gaze
into the big crystal
it almost makes your eye
drop out
waiting for the mist to clear
and you choose
where to point your finger

there, you say, that one
and your laughter
shrieking
it's your turn now

Light

But the light burns
the wind has blown out the fire
but the light is there
Pressed into earth
ready for planting
who can say
'This is wood
this is fire'?
This is
Dew on a lupin
soon gone
water wrung from
a piece of cloth
dried in the wind
Listen
This is nothingness
Who can say
'This is death'?
Who can say
'I will hold this cloud
in my hand'?
Who can say
'This is a dream'?
Time whispers into the pillow
now
Through open windows
the wind blows sunlight
into your eyes glistening
like lupins
The wind has blown away
the fire
but who can say

'Listen
This is light'?

♪

Letter from a Friend's Son

this is to say
that my father is in prison
and cannot answer letters
they keep him busy

my name is not my name
but you have met me
I am concerned
about your pale drawn face
your unshed tears
and from the packed cases
I know you're on the move again

take care they do not
catch you too
we are all spinning
in new cold power
a heavy duty formula

however many times
you read this letter
the words will change
and you will search in vain
for what you want to see
my father sends his love
he says you should read
Kleist and Eckhart
that the newspapers are torn

the lights are out

be brave and take the train
back into the darkened city

♪

You

no need
to draw blood
without thought
you said
a long time

we were
together
and the traffic
dreaming
like your hand
passing

I know you
without words
hear you
without sound
walking
without moving

I am old
last childhood
sighing
sighing
sighing

where are you
now that I
your bed
am empty?

Loving

You demand from a gallon of oil
the same.
Can you deny?

The oil gives heat
cannot love cannot
carry it carefully.

From the cold pavement
stone.

You demand the same
and my answer is yours:
treachery all promises.

But your demands are mine
so you buy oil
and carry it home
over the cold pavement.

Köln

Moments of uneasy satisfaction
cold hands in wet winds
the lake made in bad times
by hungry men.
A swan contented with her eggs
nesting in dead beech leaves.
Learned professors in galoshes
questions not understood
and answers.

♪

Anya's Winter Landscape

her horizon
sky
deepening orange
the snow shining
glass panes
the window frame

her hand
holding back the curtain
grows smaller
she sees a picture postcard
gothic roofs
dark trees
glowing sky
childhood
Moscow in technicolour

the room

cluttered with knick knacks
in different shoes
she could be anywhere
but here
each day shrinking

her world
the window frame
shrinking
in the fading afternoon

♪

The Gypsy

I would have followed you
to learn the colour of your voice
the shape which love falls into
and what it is we ask
but cannot give.

Vibrations changing with a smile
glasses filled and raised
blue eyes, brown eyes
above the smoke of people's cigarettes.

I would have followed you
where the wind crosses the moors
or the sea rises and breaks
against your shore,
but your hand in mind is every hand
and the hours become disintegrated patterns
the days silent
leaving only white trails of cloud.

You are gone.
Soon it will be last year.

♪

Coming to Egypt

I shall stand naked and weeping
my tomb just finished
the paintings hardly dry
and embalmers waiting
with iron hooks to draw my brain
while the years roll
towards no shore

what is the good then
of loving
when you lie bound and still
in the hot darkness?

it was the same
when the Nile
lapped against the pillars
of your house
and your feet
had crumbled in their sandals

♪

Last Thoughts of the Little Mermaid

There is nothing left
but to plunge deep
until the blood

licks my feet.
With the same knife
the mother of destruction
cut out my tongue.

She was wise.
Food for the sea
anyway, she said,
pain like swords
and jealousy of human love
can you bear
to win a soul?
She knew the end
would be destruction.

No, leave him sleeping
holding his love
against his heart.
Perhaps, before the sea
dissolves a choking moment,
I'll know the roundness
of the earth
and, understanding, the
grey wash of waves
will bring tears
to these liquefying
sea-grey eyes.

Andromeda

In uncertain weather
half Spring
half Winter

you, who had never left me,
came
with winged sandals
holding out your hand and
asking questions to which you knew the answers.

And I, who had never left you,
chained to a rock of myths
felt the water swirling
closing
round me.

We are one,
you said.

I saw the monster die
and where it sank in blood
sprang coloured plants.

Why then do I dream
I am held in massive jaws
and you lie beside me
turned to stone?

♪

Fishing

because you were catching crayfish
I lay beneath the red trees
chipmunks knocking down acorns
dead leaves tangled in my hair

I was alone
but you stood by me

an army of grasses
sharp under your bare feet

your white hands
detached from your body
spread across my eyes

your arms were branches
your sun-eyes blazing
as you swiftly caught me
under a glass jar
whispering gently:
no need to fear
I will be there
when you die
and the crayfish
watching from the muddy stream
put out their claws
to touch the smooth glass sides

♪

They

we are held in a tunnel of music
with magnetic walls
they have caught us

they show us a picture of a garden
which is at the end of the tunnel
it makes us cry for beauty
they say moon moon
and wrap the trees in misty shawls
they hang icicles on the branches
and sing to comfort us

they tell us we are free

sometimes they smile
and mutilate us with love
at each breath
we are growing smaller
because we are packed so tightly

we are dying to reach the garden
they are glad to have good manure
and take whips to drive us faster

♪

Summer Funeral

rain
and sweetness from damp
elm leaves

you
half smiling
in a circle
within a square

I touch you
as the rain touches
the elm leaves

you put me
in an invisible coffin
wreathed in cherry blossom
wreathed in hawthorn
wreathed in wisteria

the weeks passing like
wistful mourners

cover me
with this night's moment

♪

February

we lie together
and it is Winter
the rain falling
for centuries
for centuries
on black branches
buds on black branches

we lie entwined
in the cold room
hearing nothing
but our own sighs

and outside
people walk
huddled against the wind

♪

The Pilgrimage

six in the morning
again morning
and rain on the window

the great bell of Chartres
has swallowed me
come come come
you are no pilgrim
your feet passing over my flagstones
are like other feet
which have passed
you are my chimes

weakling weakling
you are afraid
caw the crows perching
in the cherry tree
it is time to move
time to move

you have no choice
throbs the bell
you are claimed
found out
now you must follow

we will come with you
caw the crows
grazing my head
with their wings

♪

One Thought

Each day brings me
closer to where
the horseman watches
still hidden by

flowering branches.
When Autumn strips them
I shall see the horse
black and silent
patiently waiting for
the signal to canter.

♪

The Romanies in Town

let us leave the place, brother
it is not for us
they have built a great city
with broken glass
see how it shimmers in the evening light?
their feet are bleeding
through walking on splinters
they pretend not to notice

they have offered us a house
with cabbages in the garden
they tell us of their strange country
and want us to stay
and help them fight for it

do not listen, brother
they will bind you with promises
and with hope
on all sides stretch fields of rubble
they say we should admire the view

the young are busy building
new glass palaces

they gather up the splinters
and bathe their feet with tears

come quick come quick
we will take the road towards the sea
we will pick blackberries
from hedges in the lanes
we will pitch camp on empty moors
and watch the hawk skimming
above the trees
but if we do not fight
the hawks will die, sister
they have no time for wild birds
and will shoot us down

♪

Going Home

the stairs go
to the ground floor
we say good-night
and thank you for having us
we walk down to the first floor
our footsteps are different
our moods vary
the stairs go on and on
down years and years

in New York there are carpets
in Berlin polished wood
in Paris marble
in London stairs smell
of disinfectant

we go out into the street
the houses stand
like cardboard cut-outs
the moon is near
it hangs sullenly
above the chimneys

we hurry towards the bus stop
hands in our pockets
the air is heavy
our noses blocked with soot
we look at the pavement
not at each other

when there were gods
they looked out over the valley
across the plains
they were taller than trees
they had no pockets

♪

Eurydice

My feet do not touch the damp path
winding upwards through spirals of rock
and jagged stalactites.
Gentle wind brushes my hair
blows through your cloak.

Five steps behind you always
it was your lyre you loved
did you ever know the colour of my eyes?
I was a shadow even then.

When I died your tears were songs
each one more perfect than the last
the earth mourned its very roundness
almond blossom wept with falling snow.
Outside, high on the mountains
is the great plain with wild flowers
wild flowers and air so fresh
one's head goes light.
You'll reach it first, then turn
to look at me, your lyre already singing
how your love moved Hell.
You will not see me go
shadows make no sound.

♪

On the Sea Shore

with his knife my twin
cuts a pattern on my breast
he knows that I am blind

he puts a stick in my hand
and commands me to follow
he says: this is a rock
and this a shell
the seagulls are seagulls
first things come first
do not try to run

I can hear the waves roll in
and birds shrieking overhead
I can feel the space around us

my twin says: the gentle lark
is made of cast iron
we walk in daydreams
we are blown by the wind
our branches torn
he says: the heather is purple

I try to walk
my feet sink in the sand
I cry: brother, where are you?

Eurydice in Hades

For Alberto de Lacerda

he once sang to me, saying:
'never go near the spring by the white cypress
for the water is not for you'

the house is like a cave
vast and cold
he is no longer with me

I must find the lake inside my head
walk by it quietly, listening to the thrush which sings
almost as sweetly as he did

once, I saw a frog half swallowed by a snake
the frog scrabbles at the bank, desperate,
but it was well and truly caught

like me, like him and me
caught in coils which we have made
and neither of us gods
to the guardians of my lake
I plead: 'I am a child of Earth and Starry Heaven
but my race is of Heaven alone
let me drink from
the cold water of memory
for I am thirsty and dying'

so, he taught me

will he follow me singing, or shall I follow him?
the coils unravelled at last by our own making

No Answers

in the clear light
of the first day
will there be a reason
for wanting a reason
to believe in the first day?

and on the eighth day
will fear come
three-headed
with protruding teeth
and in its brown light
will there be a reason for sorrow?

after the ninth day
is Hell a magistrates' court
where pain is encouraged
and death is impossible?

we do not know
do not not know
drawn out of time
towards time
held close by the revolving womb

the rising smoke
seems like an illumination

Bye-laws

the lady walks in the garden
her arm round the unicorn
she tells the magpies
that her life is embroidered in sunlight
why not join her?
it is forbidden to walk on the grass

no explaining
one piece of rope is as good as another
affection is a purring against legs
penalty for improper use
three months' imprisonment

moss grows on the roof
plants grow in the wall
the days come in and go out
with the tide
do not spit

we store facts
we get through examinations
we try to grow up
we can become company directors
it is an offence to travel
without a ticket

there are all makes of cages
even one like a chair
we can be quite comfortable
it is forbidden
to lean out of the window

this head which is a skull
these hands which are bones for anatomy notes

this skeleton body is sometimes happy
there comes a point of rejection
for practically everything
it is forbidden
to pass beyond these doors
no loitering

Warning

remember
when you sit
inactive
changing the world
mostly blind
this is a home for
terminal patients

Wanderlust

the organ-grinder tramps on
under iron sky
from black hills towards black mountains
I travel with him

into towns of twisted chimney pots
overhead railways a chaos of wires
rats lurking round dustbins
and out again on vast roads
the journey endless

sometimes we stop in quiet villages
and to his old tunes the people dance
with a wild joy
that fades at twilight and they remember
to bolt the doors against strangers

footsteps on gravel
footsteps on snow
the moments of monkeys are short-lived

why do you watch me organ-grinder?
why do you compel me to follow you
through these desolate forests
your music gives me no peace?

♪

Psyche

when he flew away
rising up so that I couldn't touch him

the lamp
blown out by his rushing wings
had burnt my betrayal into his flesh
I knew then that the last errand
would be the last errand

now I sit here wearily
hardly caring that the bracken and moss
are soft beneath me
hardly caring that I have come lightly
through the black and gold
there is too much time
too much left for reflection
pity is not lawful
for those hands clutching at my dress
there could only be perpetual drowning
the fierce river raging over bleak rocks
the two-headed dog, the whips and threats
all lie where the sun shines brightest

I fold these clouds around me
clouds which are really dreams
dreams which have been prohibited
and in this last defiance
dare not beg again for mercy

if he should come back
having understood what love is
will he wipe the grey dew from my face
touching me slowly gently
so that my awakening
will not be my death?

Heimweh

a thrush sings
every evening
in the ash tree

it has been singing
for as long
as I can remember
only then
the tree was probably
an oak

the song
aches and aches
in the green light
if I knew
where it was
I would go
home

♪

Love Song

enclosed world
your traffic
encroaching
on our dreams

possessions packed
in boxes
in boxes
more possessions

damp park
people shrouded
their hearts' cry
hidden
from themselves

you said once
you'd make the sun
shine for me
if you could

only now
do I believe you

Collage

Strangers came
during early Spring
they wore black coats
against the cold

Only four strangers
it was four too many
always in the woods
in the church
along the bridle path
staring across the fields

We grew anxious
called in our children
bolted the doors
counted the silver

Why had they come?
no one had asked them
what did they want?
they never said

The days quiet
apart from the winds
which whipped our cheeks
as we were ploughing
we found ourselves waiting
an emptiness round us
It was the child
who broke the spell
crept out one morning
to search for primroses
forgot the grey shapes
half hidden by the trees

One of us saw him
running breathless
down the avenue
towards the downs
at last a speck of white

Why? cried his mother
banging her head against the stones
why? she wept
into her hands

Summer came late
we hardly noticed
quarrelling among ourselves
hoarding our cherries
protecting our strawberries

Our village was never the same
gradually changing
beyond recognition
new houses, a factory
we were soon encased

And the strangers?
had they gone or stayed?
sidled in as it were
integrated
we couldn't tell

♪

June 1971

sun on the dustbins
everywhere a film of dust
and heavy smell of petrol

Summer morning in the back streets
of Brixton
birds can be heard
and traffic

jasmine flowering
over a brick wall

a person of no fixed abode
watching cigarette smoke drift
into a tree

In the Library

toothless
they come for romance
mauve hands fumbling with tickets
loud complaints
whispered confidences
they crouch among the shelves

outside
the everlasting rain

The Chariot

To Patrick White

I doubt it will arrive on a grey day.
The clouds must part a little and
streaks of red, pale salmon, watery blue
appear in the interval before night.

And it will not come near towns.
It will not crash through the fragile
icing of sponge cakes or bone china
or the uncertainties of plastic doilies,
modern conveniences, civilised living.

But our mirrors will be shattered,
fall away in tiny crystals.
Mirrors of water too. Ruffled
by sand churned up as the horses
gallop forward laying bare the light behind
the eyes. Eyes which are clear.

And there must be silence.
To hear the far-off hoof beats
the swift turning of the glowing wheels.

Anne! Sister Anne!

From the fairy story 'Bluebeard'

I see the sun making dust
and the grass growing green.
Our house is one of many in a road
we've lived in too long.
My sisters' faces shine in the window
they called me to be near them on this sultry afternoon.

In front of the house is a patch of grass
and one flower bed with black soil –
hollyhocks grow there and later straggly chrysanthemums.
The privet is cut low, the step well scrubbed.
It's quiet in this no man's land
where we have returned from different places.

Waiting at the foot of the stairs
is a dog, he wags his tail in greeting
as I drift up towards the room
where we have hidden past belongings –
a book with pictures no one would explain
a bracelet which was lost on a dreary day
and words which are kept in dusty boxes –
but the room is empty, and noises don't penetrate
these walls. This is where I dropped
the blood-stained key.
                    In the distance
I see a cloud which could be a flock
of sheep or two horsemen –
it is a long way off.

In Transit

This is the point of departure
or return.
For the moment past and future events
assume a relevance
which could be classified as madness.

That I was born cannot be denied
my parents called it an afterthought,
in any case I have emerged
from the cocoon of blood which is our birth rite.

Someone is practising the piano
the music floats upwards
Chopin, Bach, jazz
it varies according to the musicians
who vary constantly.

Outside the window is a cherry tree
its branches are near enough to pick
the ripe fruit which is delicious.

My grandmother is knitting
the ash from her cigarette grows longer
and longer.
My grandfather's room smells of snuff
the stairs, the hall and the landing also
smell of snuff.

The family brings me toys
clockwork clowns, tops, a teddy bear
they lie discarded in the garden
where the evening mist is rising

willow trees just visible in the grey haze.
A time when the soul
is most vulnerable.

I am thinking of a lace bird
sewn over a scorch mark on a dress
and a tiny basket filled with marigolds;
the others in the garden don't remember
it means as little to them as the milk cart
which delivers our milk.

The rhododendrons have been cut down
so has the cedar tree
the spinney has been cleared to build new houses
the garden is unrecognisable.

Like the faces – sad faces
eyes glistening, but not tears
signs of strain, sleepless nights, overwork,
they pass my window daily
I have given up trying to name them.
Even those closest become blurred.

The days are not empty
but I keep within the confines of these walls
employed in working a tapestry
which unfolds the usual accounts
of battles lost or won.

A young girl passes
she carries a shopping basket and a bunch of flowers
I look for a sign of recognition
but she refuses to give it.
Downstairs a hired assassin is eating
homemade bread and jam –
it is of no importance.

The stream of traffic gets heavier
fighting has broken out in the streets
people are afraid to walk alone after dark
we have progressed to another century.

♪

Distance

We were friends years ago –
walking to school along respectable streets,
touching, smelling all that suburbs have to offer.
We shared friends the same way we shared sweets.
Sometimes we quarrelled.
London kept us slightly distant.

In the country we had a deeper communion.
For hours we sat by streams, silent,
to hear the gurgling of water
on stones and dried leaves.
We lay, on sunny days, among thyme and rosemary.
Stole red-currants, which hung,
like an Aunt's necklace, on green threads.

The antics of adults puzzled us.
Fascinated we watched them balancing
tea-cups on floral knees,
sprinkling fruit cakes with sugar,
downing whisky or dabbing perfume.
Idle days. We learnt much.
Not enough. Our years stretched unending.
We looked forward to growing. To freedom.

Back in town we played with dolls.
Witnessed mysteries and anguish we had no part in.

Went to church, over the common where seagulls
shrieked above the pond.
We discovered later that Hell yawned beneath us.

Our respectable streets shook with bombs.
It was about then – when the safety
of childhood was crumbling –
we began to part company.
A slow process. One night,
after she'd screamed out her grief
at the minor cruelties of life –
the rows, smell of whisky and vomit –
she withdrew. To a world of dreams
I thought. But perhaps I was wrong.

In any case we lost touch.
Forgot her – almost. Until this morning
I opened a book and saw her name written
clearly, in a childish hand –
and a photograph. A thin child.
Nothing remarkable. Missed her suddenly.
Remembered scrambling over rocks
looking for shells, scampering over the moors
to pick heather. Nothing remarkable.

Shut the book, and wrote on a scrap of paper:
wish you were here.

♪

Passing Moment

As she brushed her hair
she'd look in the mirror
and the strange woman peered back

curiously. Peering back
from a distance.

The family laughing in the kitchen
for once their moods in accord.
Blue patterned cups on the table
a smell of coffee and orange peel.
She recalled the scene clearly.

Here was stillness –
the floorboards creaking a little
light diminishing. The last bird song
in the garden. Hauntingly.

And the arch of the stairwell
expanding as she floated down.
Floated secretly. Those curious eyes
delving her thoughts.

Don't go further ...
behind that door forty years gone by
changes you'll never accept ...

The laughter
her hand on the door.

♪

Unposted Letter

Cathedral bells rang for Angelus.
At six I stop work, return to the quiet house
which is invariably empty –
on evenings of long rain
I'm grateful for the warmth of the familiar room.

In another season
we gazed at our own reflections
in the eyes of strangers.
This, among stubble fields and a basket of violets.
We always regret the passing of dreams.

Soon our lives will be digested
with the unrest, anger and silent railway tracks,
to appear – perhaps – in a future text book.
For emotions read romantic novels.

Those who I've parted from
are one with my body
and only when I'm dead will they drop away
free to stand alone –
or maybe, they're flaking off gradually
like particles of skin.
In the same way I, too, am flaking
gathering the particles.

Sometimes, alone, I shed tears
for actions, for certain vanities
which can't be altered,
also for children who might have been born
and for those who were born
who suffer ordinarily.

Already there are buds on the trees
on the table is a bunch of jonquils.
The red shade of the lamp glows.
Noises change subtly as the night advances.
A car passes. I hear the wind in the chimney –
occasionally voices.

Roman Comedy

In the year 14 AD Julia III died. The daughter of Augustus, she'd been imprisoned by her father for immorality. According to Tacitus she was married first to Marcus Agrippa and afterwards to Tiberius whom she despised. When he became Emperor he exiled her and let her waste away to death by slow starvation.

Stones falling away
down down
crushing the foliage
bouncing on rocks
splashing in the sea
'Take care how you tread.'

A lizard puts out its tongue
a fly vanishes.
The silence of heat.

'A little further
only a little further
don't stumble
this is a beautiful place
why be afraid?
No one lives here now.'

No soldiers stand guard
spears glinting
visors closed
eyes closed

not to see her wasted hands
scratching in the soil for roots.
Her once glorious hair
stringy, unkempt.

Who dared go against
the Emperor.

In the first months
walking at sunset
to stand on a rock
with outstretched arms.

Later, she crawled
night after night
watching the horizon
her eyes sore
hungry for rescue.

Hungry,
she raved, prowled the apartments
screamed
that she was her father's daughter
while the soldiers stared
hands uneasy on their swords.

No more lovers
no husbands
no banquets
no no no ...
as she tore at a piece of bread.

Sleeping fitfully
listening hopefully
for the steps of murderers:
finish me quickly.

But one more crust
in the morning
one more cup of water
one more ...

until the Senate were informed
of her death.

I cannot walk any further
the path's too steep
the heat too much
the sky too blue –
let me go back.

'It is a beautiful place
lizards in the crevices
the trees on the cliff side
so old and dark.'

Hold me
look at me again
I shall not return.

♪

The First Dance

She rode through
the cold morning of the world
on the back of a lioness ...
unaware of his presence ...
she was crowned with poppies
her song triumphant.
Hidden in the rocks
crouching, ready to spring,
he saw her hair gleaming in
the whirling circle of the sun ...
And the wind stirred ...
she laughed. Breaking her song,
she leapt down to watch

the rippling grass.
Then she moved her body carefully
undulating, imitating
raising her arms she moved her body
sinuous, lithe ... he marvelled,
creeping from his hiding place
feeling a hollowness
which caught his breath ...
he knew his loneliness.
He moved forwards, towards
this innermost reflection of himself ...
he moved his body fearfully
imitating, undulating
step by step ...
one hand stretched out ...
aware of his presence
crowned with poppies
she took his hand
her song echoing the reflection
of her innermost feelings
in the cold morning of the whirling sun.

♪

The Entertainers

For Michael McCormick

The clouds obscured the view,
he could just see the hedge
and burnt stubble of the field.
She moved in the bed uneasily
'So thirsty. Shrivelled.'
Filling a glass he raised her head
guiding the water to her lips.

'This bitterness will kill you.'

Faithful he'd stayed beside her
dancing, turning cartwheels, somersaults,
sweating under his chalk-white eyes
patient for signs of change.
'Is this the way I'm forced to spend my life?
Soured by your jokes.'

'It's I who weep.' She turned away her head.
'They're here again, outside. Your friends –
gypsies, circus folk. They've come to feed me.'
A light rain pattered on the roof
sparks from the logs spat into the grate
the fields cradling the house
in earth and mist.
We'll never leave.
The woman with the shadow of a clown.

♪

Miranda

He raised a storm ...
All night we watched the heaving sea
wrestle with grotesque shapes
which formed familiar patterns
in our minds.

     Closely bound. Interwoven.
     Father and daughter
     husband and wife
     companions of fantasy.
     Twelve years within the circle
     he had drawn, until at last

he was released from Caliban.
And I was free.

Since nothing can be had for nothing
you, Ariel, were the price we paid
for knowledge. My body
which is that of man and woman
could not contain you.

We still grieve your absence.
Sometimes, I see him standing
vulnerable, stretching out a hand
trying to grasp the southern breeze
which is upon your head.

♪

Andante Cantabile

Lying among lace-covered pillows
she can hear the wind blowing when she wakes –
it rattles the shutters of her room
sweeps across the oak trees in the park –
disturbs her dreams.

Two eyes
a nose
a face framed by hair
staring at a face
from a mirror framed in red velvet.

Languidly, she checks the clock
lives through her days dreaming of incidents
which never happen,
have never happened.

She transforms familiar objects
has almost learnt to turn water into wine.

'... but don't you recall? We wintered in Biarritz ...'
The flounce of her white dress brushing the grass.

The mirror always has been slightly menacing.

♪

The Condemned

On the 3rd, 6th, 9th and 40th day after the funeral, old Prussians and
Lithuanians prepared a meal to which, standing at the door, they
invited the soul of the deceased. The meal was eaten in silence and any
crumbs dropped were left for the lonely souls who had no friends or
relations to feed them. After the meal, the priest took a broom and
swept the souls out of the house saying: 'Dear souls, ye have eaten and
drunk. Go forth. Go forth.' *The Golden Bough*

Between the mountains
the sun is still glowing.
On the peaks a little snow.
Here on the pastures cows graze
not even their clanking bells
disturb the tranquillity
of late Summer.

A woman stands at the open door of the house,
she is calling to someone.
Behind her a priest
peers over her shoulder.
They wait quietly.

So, it is the fortieth day
and the table set for a feast.

Those plates are not in daily use,
the bread newly baked,
plums, golden, unblemished,
picked in the hush of the morning.
I have no appetite.
I enter the house with reluctance.
Their silence is uncanny.
Have they nothing to say
to the lonely souls
who have followed me in?
I, in turn,
have nothing to say.
Her face, tanned by the air,
has grown thinner.
Her hands tremble
as she sets the cup on the saucer.
It clatters a fraction.
She needn't fear
I will soon be gone and
have no wish for her to toss
restlessly on the pillows.
Her doom is much like ours –
lonely in the midst of loneliness,
the church bells ringing on Sundays
the long walk down to the village
clutching her rosary.
We understand her. Our silent sympathy
fills the room, with its checked curtains
its geraniums. Everything shining.

She has no appetite.
The slice of cake untouched on her plate.
If only I could tell her
what she is missing –
tell her to look out of her doorway
across the valley and see ...

Time is up, we must go forth.
The priest grows old, his bones crack
as he stoops to pick up the broom.

♪

Persephone

How long has she been in Hades?
It was immaterial,
crows were her constant companions
guarding her every move.

Tricked by six pomegranate seeds
her heart grew colder in captivity
and even during her few months' freedom
it took a long time for the sun's rays to penetrate.

Ruler, yet ruled, powerless in a domain
of police sirens. Prisoner of a devious mind.
Eternity was a tunnel through which the damned
    journeyed.
For all her secret knowledge she, too, was damned.

Whenever she saw his black horses
plunge into the gaping earth
she wondered how long it took to die.
She had never believed in immortality.

Oh, she was loved, deeply and darkly.
He had scraped her depths
until she sat gold-crowned and mute
compassion in her eyes only.

The Awakening

To Kurt Benning

1

It is a field – I suppose –
difficult to distinguish since amorphous sky
and earth merge almost colourless ...
there is no distinction between night and day
hardly any between us except for the number
which is sewn neatly on our clothes.
In the past we played a game – grandmother's footsteps –
it whiled away bleak time
until ... the silence ...
no wind
not even a sparrow chirping
although some of us recall having seen one or two
perched on the telegraph wires ...
disconnected memories haunt us
words, mainly –
these are cherished possessions, savoured voluptuously
on the tip of a tongue ...
Spring
Summer
Grass
Water ...
Speech is not denied us, but almost unnecessary
we keep closely together – for warmth and comfort.
We are waiting – I suppose ...
I have seen them once ...
they were standing in battle formation,
very beautiful in this weird half-light,

grey stones
on what could have been the horizon.

2

Most people are like a shaving of wood which is curled round its central emptiness. –
THEOPHAN THE RECLUSE

We stand in line.
None of us think further ...
this dim, cold place numbs us –
mercifully –
all mediocre souls
without courage for sin
or virtue.
We expected nothing
gave nothing
received nothing
conforming to current patterns
walking in yellow lighted streets
absorbed by our own footsteps
with no experience of joy
and suffering second-hand.

The rest of our story is in colour ...
vivid red, gold, silver
blending of painful light
enabling us to look briefly
into what had been ourselves.

We are here in line.
It is sufficient.

Four Poems for David Jones

He does what is done in many places
what he does other
          he does after the mode
of what has always been done.
          — DAVID JONES, *The Anathemata*

Thomas

Yes, I remember the stifling room
where we huddled together
afraid to go out in the street
or open a window even.
The others swear that you came.
They believed all right.
But the circumstances were out of the ordinary
our minds were confused.
At that moment I should have believed anything —
anything that would bring relief.
Now I still doubt.
I doubt that my fingers felt the wet flesh
that my eyes saw the marks on your feet and hands.
And yet I praise you.
Standing on arid ground
dying of thirst I continue to question.
My luggage is heavy.
At times my feet touch the pavement.
My body does not magnify you
but I feel your presence.
To speak the name of the dead
makes them live again,
restores the breath of life to him who has vanished.

The way is opened
and I have entered without understanding.

Blessed are they that have not seen.

The Fishermen

The water was so clear
you could see the stones at the bottom of the lake.
Little ripples splashed onto the beach
with a gentle swish, swish.
Resin from the pine trees, salt and that sweet indefinable
    smell
of a Summer night.
A bat swept past our heads.
We sat, sit, propped against the boats,
our faces aged and tired.
Another beach, another lake, another place
we've been through it all before.
Just fishermen, minding our own business
drying our nets in the sun –
there was something about his face
couldn't put it into words –
when he hired the boat we never asked for money.
Not that we listened much to what he said that day,
probably nobody else did either,
we went on drying our nets, sweat trickling down our
    backs.

These days we don't do much fishing,
we're growing old, grumbling towards our graves,
we've not all died in glory.
The young ones come along, sit at our feet
questioning, arguing, sceptical, take notes.

They're always clamouring for miracles
and never get the joke about old Peter
jumping into the water with all his clothes on.
We had our bellyful of miracles
until we almost learnt that just living is enough.
We might have known
that being reborn is no easy matter.

Mary of Magdala

The final integration
or disintegration
I never distinguished which
of my soul
took place, it seemed to me,
on a fine afternoon
at that arch in the middle of the High Street,
the one with the pots of geraniums
where you get a view of the sea on a clear day.
I connected the feeling
which was rooted in my navel
with that of a fertile ovary.

Standing still, seeing the incomparable beauty
of the dirty cobblestones,
having traced the body of man
in intricate design on many a bed
and being responsible for this and much more,
I gathered the parts of my disjointed life
to reach a point beyond my comprehension.

In tranquillity I lie among them that are on fire.

Nicodemus

Keeping a sense of proportion
lip service to what is considered correct
I have brought what is needed to bury the dead.
Once again I come to you by night.
This time to take away all visible proof of my
    understanding.
In secret I have applied myself
to seek out wisdom
to know what is before my face –
the inside and the outside are reversed
that which is
has become that which is not –
displaced, troubled
I live naked in a house that is not my own
and the five trees of Paradise evade me.

The Comforter

This morning, admiring a newly opened rose,
his shadow crept over my shoulder
and the birds uttered warning cries.
A reminder that my country is far away
time to begin the journey home.
I have grown fond of this place
this enclosed garden
with overgrown roses and clustered wisteria,
my many loves,
but he has revealed himself in dreams
his embrace is comforting.

        He has followed me through the streets,
        sat near me in the train,
        behind me in my room.
        Always loving,
        since my birth he has observed my growing,
        looked closely into my living.
        Always impartial.

The rowan berries shine in the setting sun
clouds are gathering across the fields.
Days drop with the leaves
are trodden into the earth – vanish.
When I ask him 'Now?'
he ruffles my hair with long fingers.
He waits.
High time to start back, a long walk,
and much will have changed.

From the Duke's Book of Hours

January

Stars obscured by snow clouds.
Scent of pine cones burning.
The year just begun and struggling
with resolutions which won't be kept
because soon Spring will be talked of
something to look forward to
the worst of the weather yet to come.
Snow falling, settling on the window panes.
Fortunate he who sits by his hearth
on such a night ...

February

The snow
soaked through my shoes.
Tender he was: 'Go, warm yourself
by the fire. Your little feet
are like ice. I'll draw the water.'
And I left him
in the yard –
the crows were feeding, croaking greedily.
He looked ridiculous
with a sack thrown
over his head, his big boots
sticking out on spindly legs.
Reminded me of the young
peach tree by the fence
spindly, stark in this Winter light
yet will bear unbelievable pink blossom.

Marriage was a dream. Not a kitchen
hearth, my hands chapped
the work heavy
my belly heavy with child
and will be for years.
Me the goodwife
with my skirt pulled up to my knees
my goodman trudging to work
in the biting wind –
our faces illuminated momentarily
by a gift of God.

March

Patiently these stained-glass replicas
bend their backs to the relentless months.
Planting or hoeing beneath the watchful
but protective walls.
New life stirs again, skylarks soar into
blue air. Messengers arrived from
other places to report on cruel landlords
more homeless on the roads. Revolutions, murders,
not our concern.
We love this ploughed and neatly furrowed earth.
Placid days. Our nights punctuated by the hissings
and whisperings of the snakes as they coil
and recoil in the foundations of the house.

April

How can I sing her praises?
My voice is pure because her eyes have looked in mine.
She is my soul and I shall fear no evil.

Primroses carpet the ground, violets fall
from her parted lips. Her eyes reflect
the lapping water – clear as the skies above us.
The fishermen have cast their nets, the fish
leap to her command.
We have exchanged rings.
We have made our vows.
Her fragile face. Her gentle laughter.

May

You'll never forget
these happy days of bewilderment
fragile blossoms trembling under
cynical hands.
No one will hurt a hair of your golden head –
the veil arranged just so.
The trees cast odd shadows
on the soul's dominion and dreams are not
so easily shattered as you'd suppose – like wine
they help to dull the pain. It happens.
Ask me, who have watched more than one procession
pass by, ask me lying here among
the sick and dying, the stench almost bearable
as I dream of hyacinths.

June

A representative of the peasants
this man and his scythe are one.
The slow swing of the arms, perfect rhythm
of movement. Brilliant sunlight on the fields
he sees nothing, he only feels the ice-cold sweat

cooling his burning skin. And his wife,
who sings softly as she rakes the hay
into tidy mounds, is a shadow lost in the sun.

July

Sunflowers and olives.
An olive grove where a woman
kneels to her work. Black scarfed.
No joy in her carved face –
resentment flashes as holiday-makers
pass in the sunlight, careless. Laughing.
'I must work.'
Oil and wine blessed by ripples
of salt on the neat border of sunflowers.
Yellow papery heads, the tough
stems stretching up through olive eyes.
Black and golden kneeling under the trees
oil of gladness
oil of regeneration
flowing through her weary hands.

August

Three roads cross
by the old yew tree
three moons shine
on the golden apples
one grain of wheat
in the palm of a hand
one hair threaded
in a fine needle.

With sweet herbs
and belladonna
I fly to meet you
your lips stained
by the Lammas wine,
and two beating hearts
are knotted in the soft
wax of my arms.

September

In the chalky dust
of the square
some men play bowls.
It is cooler now.
The women coming slowly home
their donkeys staggering
under the weight of baskets
filled to the brim
with grapes.
A voice raised in the calm evening
and the piercing cry of a child.
Only the crumbling walls
and the great plane trees
stay to tell the tale.

October

A fine view from the hill
sloping fields shelter the town
smoke curls in the keen air
and leaves red as flames
floating, withering

fit for a grave.
Reality isn't only the flash
of a woodpecker's wing
it is also the warmth
of a melting embrace
there is more than one truth.
Speech may be difficult
silence unlikely
in the heart of the fire.
Death comes as it wills.

November

Life will continue
to the end
which could be bitter.
Never 'enough'
always more
pain being manifold
and some broken
sleep-walking through
slanting rain
their work carried into eternity
leaving no mark
no void.

December

It was towards evening
he walked out of the sun
he could have been a pilgrim.
The dogs didn't bark
as he lifted the latch of the gate.

He said he was going home
pointing to the mountains.
He asked for water.
Now the trees sway
in the east wind
and the morning's frosty
snow on the hills.
I keep thinking how his eyes searched
and smiled
and his hand delicate
on the cup of freshly
drawn water.

And I think
as I stir the fire
or peel potatoes
how there have only been one or two
illuminated moments
in my life
the rest is nothing.

The Fall

Two people creep from their iron towers
and search for scraps
there are no fish in the sea
no apples on the trees
no wheat in the fields
a serpent lies dying with the lambs
and iron girders circle the earth.

The sorrowful figure
standing in the corner of the painting
is about to close the gates.
No one will leave this garden.

St Michael and the Dragon

They wrestled all night
without bloodshed
he has no choice
but to ascend.
They have achieved
a perfect balance
expressing
their acceptance.
He whispers
follow me.

The moon fades
the granite rocks
grow visible
spike by spike.

Christ Tempted by the Devil

The bread
suicide
even the filigree castles
of dreams
meant little.
The real test would come
when the drops of sweat
fell on the rough grass
the cicadas singing out the desolate night
while his friends slept.

In Nunhead Cemetery

A half-mile walk in the late afternoon
cold rain, darkening sky
even the daffodils
fail to assure him of approaching Spring.

His daily constitutional
rain, sun or snow
down overgrown paths, past family vaults
jays shrieking in the trees ...

Fifty years ago she fell asleep
in his arms
twisting a gold curl in a feverish hand
her eyes staring beyond him
as if she could see the ivy
tangled round a headless angel
above her grave ...

Sarah Emilia
his young bride
asleep before she was awake
mourned by the dank moss
his tears dry.

Diploma

Virgo without a rising sign
The day – Monday
The month – September
The time – forgotten
It rained just before breakfast
And the man, no great hero,
loved his wife, promising her things
which in the end
amounted to misunderstandings

Beyond the wood,
said grandmother,
is a road
rocky, deserted
nothing grows there
a few birds skim
never lingering
Take care
to avoid it

The world,
said grandfather,
is an exciting place
I've travelled everywhere
in Russia the snow
would have covered you
Men, said mother, are liars
Women, said father, never tell the truth

The Amazon is in South America,
said teacher,
yellow and blue make green

Napoleon came from Corsica
You, child, are an imbecile

Don't cry
don't speak to me like that
don't be naughty
don't fidget
Watch the birdie,
said grandfather
And took a photograph

Interrogation

The methods hardly vary
only the questions you ask yourself
until you break
not on Friday
not even Saturday
but much later
when it is too late to step back
your whispers will formulate
the answers

The Courtship

I am curiously stirred
by the landscape
as I wait lazily for
my lover
lazily in the hot sun

no hurry
life goes on
time to admire
my long thin arms
they blend with
the long thin grass
their frailty is deceptive
my lover will not be the first
to know their strength

strange to consider
how small he always is
true, he moves gracefully
but never quick enough

when he is joined to me
too absorbed to notice
my knife-like grip
I will eat him inch by inch
I'll not need another meal
for many hours

afterwards I will sit quietly
under the exotic leaves
raising my arms again
as if praying

Day Duty

The cuckoo, doctor, is my alarm clock in the Summer.
Without moving from the bed, at his first call,
I see the garden quivering expectantly,
freshly damp – a world renewed.
I lie amazed at such perfection.

The cat, doctor, is the bell for breakfast,
ever insistent, her amber eyes fixed on mine,
her claws sharpened to receive the contents of a tin.
And all the time the birds chattering;
I move slowly, surely, gathering momentum to face the day.

Such an efficient system.
The bees, doctor, are my example.
Monotonous buzzing, bumbling in and out the startling
        colours.
The moorhen's eggs have hatched and
the swallows glide from the boiler house.
It all runs according to the plan.

Yes, doctor, give me your draught
of forget-me-nots and orange flower,
The patients in my care are too sane, too logical.
I need the long, cool drink
which leaves my mind in heaven,
my body in a state of fine imbalance.

Night Duty

The scud has crossed the heath
enveloping everything in clammy breath.
I can just make out the shape of a horse on the roof
and a mammoth grazing on the lawn.
The time between day and night
last chirrupings, daisies curled, a pheasant's
squawk from somewhere in the field.
Lights on in the village.
Reporting for duty in the TV room, doctor.

Each piece of furniture is alone
isolated where the floorboards creak without being trodden
    on.
Incantations are useless. Let the blood be,
it flows like water from the gutter.
Photographs on a screen.
Shadows on a screen.
The moon comes up behind the willow tree.
On watch. Bemused. Stunned.

To Those who Sleep in Dust

And the sun
sets peacefully
behind the pine trees
the sky growing deep
deeper
till it has swallowed the last
tip of grass

And we close our eyes
trusting
that we shall be able to open them
we walk trustingly
into the arms of our executioners
we walk lightly
on the blood-spattered pavements
we obey commands of others
who also trust others
who trust they are right
and the earth
trembles, pales

And the sun shines
how it shines, warms,
transforms the dust
into shimmering sparks
the smoke into blue shreds of clouds
pushes its soft fingers
through the cold flesh
to touch the marrow of cold bones

Non-Happening

Neither to blame.
A momentary loss of control
on both sides.
The encounter could almost be called
radiant, for one of them.
Left – an afternoon of sunshine,
a few hours of discussion
and a handprint
burning into her flesh.

♪

The Great Man is Dead

For Anna Dostoievsky

When he lay dying he worried
about the fate of his family:
'What am I leaving you with, my dearest?
My poor girl, how will you live?'
As always his wife soothed him.
He died peacefully.

She survived.
Long enough to bring up his children,
publish his collected works,
found a school in his name,
compile a bibliography, sort letters, papers
and see them placed in a new museum.
She wrote and re-wrote her story of their marriage.
A deathly survival. It kept her sane.

At the funeral, someone remembered seeing her –
draped in black, heavily veiled,
befitting a modest widow. Two children at her side.
A touching picture.

All the devotion, self-sacrifice, love
ended years later, in a cold room.
She died painfully.
Was he with her, in spirit, to comfort
her last hours?
There was no one else.
She was his wife. Nothing more.
Nothing less.

♪

The Captive

Based on a Russian folk tale

Back and forth
along the shore
of this deserted beach
disconsolate
her dress wet round the hem
billowing in the wind
like her hair
tangled
salt sprayed.
This, the one place
where she can walk freely
never free of the rocky house
perched so crazily on the cliff side
never free of the love
which led to this prison.

'Inviolable,' he'd say, laughing,
'my name is Deathless.'
She kicked against the stones
where did he keep his death?
In a kernel
in a nut
in a worm
on a shrub
in a garden
inaccessible?

'Tell me, my dear,
your secret.
The bones of my pursuers
lie dry and clean
on the road to this fortress.
But I have talked with
the winds and the sea
my strength is failing.
I dream of your hands smoothing my hair
I dream of your voice soothing my fears.
In the daylight
I hear your laughter echoing
in the high chimneys
and I see my own reflection
in the polished wood of the table.'

Narcissus

He saw a new aspect of himself
transfigured for a moment
by his brilliant eyes

Becoming whole
he heard his sorrowful echo
echo:
I love you
you

♪

The Collector

For Peter Kaplan

Grey the stone
the sky
your basket dragging
your steps
back from the grocer
the butcher
the candlestick maker
under the clouds
rain
sometimes sun

at the street corner
scatter the light-footed
the tender, all
those whose turn has come
to ride upon the winds from North or South
East or West

Grey your face
grey your clothes
lonely
walking through the front door
of your grey life

little island
isolated
in the bay
of your window

is this it, then?
a kind of discarding
skin of a snake
shed for collectors
to place on the shelf
gathering dust?

Living is a grey matter
in the mind

The children are playing
catch me if you can Mr Wolf
but supper time is a long way off
They are searching
among stained shadows
mud splattered

They sing an old song
of wild birds
and snake calls
and the word's flutter of scarlet

Their front doors are closing
stone upon stone
blocks the bay of the window

The collector has turned
to dust on the shelf

Modern Fairy Tale

Once, not long ago,
a princess lived in a tower
at Factory Junction.
Locked up by a kind of Black Magic.

When she looked out of the window
she could see the railway lines
the gas works and Battersea Power Station.
Her prince came to visit her
as all princes have always done
at night.
He didn't have to climb her hair
she went whirling down from the eighteenth floor
in a lift.

Horses, known to them both from TV
were not practical.
They used a motor bike.

She never danced her shoes to pieces
he never found a dog in a walnut shell
they never knew if they were in love
but as they tore through Battersea
he would think, vaguely, of taking her away
somewhere.

Neither of them realised
that escape was impossible,
and when they sat together in the Wimpy Bar

they talked of living in another tower
on the other side of the river.

There is no end to this story.

♪

In Defence of La Belle Dame Sans Merci

She has searched so long
she's even begun to wonder what it is she searches for
illusions everywhere she turns.

All those knights in shining armour
pale and dying for want of her
are no more true than their loving protestations.
Their milk-white steeds just cars
in which she's driven back and forth
admiring different aspects of London life.
Goddess, Nymph, a Faery's Child – mere names.
Her elfin grot a flat with views of other flats,
her children spread around the world.
And when she weeps: 'I love you true'
she, too, means it for a while.

Dust caked on the broken pavements
geraniums growing in grimy windows
someone said: 'I hope you'll be happy,'
as he slammed the door. And another said:
'What makes you think because I'm young
I have more hope than you?'

Deserted under a railway arch she dreams of
cancerous growths, deformities, tramping feet
and wailing voices.

Why blame her for her dancing foot
her flowing hair, wild eyes?
She roams, listless, by withered sedge and lake
afraid that the end of disillusion
is only another lie.

♪

Sequel to Some Fairy Tales

They were happy.
They were happy.
He carried her away to his castle.

From a distance
in the warm Summer night
set among trees and daisy-covered fields
it did resemble fairyland.
Not a delicate structure
but moated, built with massive walls and towers,
where, after the second winter,
she shivered and declined.
He had troubles, too.
The land, it seemed, belonged to someone else.
His father had omitted to tell him of the mortgage.
Besides he was oversensitive,
the harsh life, overseeing of criminals
tortures, executions, did not agree with him.
He became morose. Then manic.
At times taking to the woods
he'd howl like an animal in pain.

Who speaks now?
It is I, Marie. Wife of my lord.
Unhappy wife. I looked into the dark

and found no comfort there.
Secret.
Secret is my soul
the walls hold death.
He came quiet and terrible.
All fairy tales finished.

The castle fell to ruins.
Still crumbles.
On warm Summer nights,
calm nights
he whirls out of the stillness
tearing at the walls
howling her name –
leaving an equal stillness in his wake.

♪

Orpheus Arrives in a New World

In order to enter the temple
it is necessary to lift aside the second veil.
It would be easier, Orpheus thought, in another country.
Here, all things flourished
whether he sang or no.
The rivers were broader and longer
the trees were taller, mosquitoes fiercer
and even the crows spoke a different language.

He put his lyre in a locker at the bus station
and walked into town.
He peered in the wide cracks of paving stones
examining the usual amounts of dirt encrusted there.
He gazed in the windows of broken-down houses
admired decrepit elegance, imagining days gone by –

imagining ladies, particularly ladies, with parasols,
lace hankies clutched in little hands,
gleaming teeth, gleaming hair under beribboned bonnets.

He loved them all.
Blew kisses through the torn curtains.

An old man sheltering in a porch,
a bottle to his lips, nuzzling with soft gulps,
observed Orpheus as he smiled and bowed
blowing kisses to an unseen audience.
The old tramp laughed and spat:

'Why don't you sing, Orpheus?
This is Hell.'

In order to enter the temple
it is also necessary to pass between the pillars.
Orpheus, hands in pockets
striding through the dead leaves.
Orpheus, uninspired, stalking through
browns and yellows, taking note
of sounds, colours, sights and smells.
Scowling, his voice tuneless.

He found Eurydice in the kitchen.
His goddess, sitting between the pillars
of sink and gas stove.
'I am the great law,' said Orpheus.
And the woman turned her face to look at him.

Echo of Conscience

'These children put us to shame, whilst we slumber, they set forth gaily.' – POPE INNOCENT III *on the Children's Crusade*

Dust flew up in clouds
and the clouds over their heads
butterflies
shimmering in hysterical song.

A knot of poverty in the pit of the stomach
they set out for the kingdom of God.
It was the best thing that had happened
to some of them –
leaving the villages
and the knots of parental obedience
which left scars on protruding bones.

At first there was bread, even wine,
prayers, praise and much curiosity –
especially in the soft, supple bodies.
The last chaste knot to be tied or untied.
Naked love would conquer the infidel
since the sword could not.
And the infidel were butterflies
gaudy, exotic. And they were animals
tamed, gentle, miraculously following
the children. Full of trust in their faithfulness.

Many of the children were thrown into brothels
or sold into slavery.
Some returned later
faith washed off in blood.

And they needed the miracles, the butterflies

to snatch their souls from bitterness.
Most of them died.

♪

Unholy Giving

Based on a spell: How to understand what the birds are saying

Split leaves
and rotting fungus underfoot
the dogs sniffed out the prey

For you alone
I cooked and such a heart
which cost long nights
I ate
and later heard the pheasant
speak clearly to the sparrow

Dear love, my first kiss was to give you pleasure
For you alone I broke the Fast
If I kiss you twice,
like Eve, I want to share
the unacceptable

♪

Leiston Abbey

Through the refectory
open to the setting sun,
the grass wet, muddy in places
near the chiselled flint,

they passed. Soundlessly,
heads covered, hands concealed,
hugging the walls, to pray
in the Lady Chapel – which remains
intact but locked.
In the peace of old stones
is carved a rabbit, ears portrayed
by streaks of white, the back smooth
beautifully rounded, shoots of grass
growing over the folded paws.
There are the two of us and stillness.
The stone moves gently
as though a heart were beating quickly.
And bending down I see that the stone
is alive and suffering.
This is its sanctuary.
Nothing makes sense
with the heavy clouds spitting rain
onto the rabbit, its eyes obliterated
by the large swellings of diseased flesh.

♪

The Visitor

Based round a spell on how to conjure
three people into your room when lonely

Three people came
you stayed
Love would be shameless
if disintegration were not final

When you have eaten the bread,
drunk the water,

simple things
asked for simply
come near me and
I will study the lines
of your face
the shape of your finger-nails
nothing more

I will juggle
with swallows
for you
with colours of geraniums
with sea spray
of a minute universe
in the hours of Mercury
in the minutes of June

No law against
your voice
in the hours of Saturn
in the minutes of January
and the longing for you
undiminished
cherished
now I am invisible

Through this window pane
the pear tree
point in sudden space
the alien days
gnarled and blossoming

nameless your presence
in this white-washed room
solitary this bed

Candlemas

Candles.
Stone pillars waver and glow
with tiny flames.

This is the time for recollection,
for sowing of seeds
veneration of virgins
a coming of day
a looking forward.

In what do we believe?
I find no answer.
For what do we pray?
Metanoia?

We are part
of a skilful tapestry
reflecting the moving year.

♪

Gossip

Snow.
Thick snow.
A partridge spied on by a pheasant
searches for food.
The pheasant is closely observed
by the farmer's boy –
he has a gun.
Unknown to him the secret police
are very interested in his movements.

The villagers, naturally curious,
fish for red herrings
in the frozen pond.

♪

September Fable

The soldiers were tired,
coming out from the city
in the crazy heat
to look for a man.

And there was this gardener
watering his strawberries
tending his carrots
bringing his grapes
to the table, his wine.
Sharing his supper.

He told them:
'Tomorrow. Always put off
till tomorrow what could
be done today. Eat now,
be merry, there's plenty of time
for a killing. Tomorrow
I'll show you your man.'

Come morning he stands
with dew on his feet
by a grave dug as carefully
as his asparagus bed.
'Bury me here alongside
my carrots and strawberries.
I am your man.'

The soldiers are sad.
Coming back from the village
blood on their minds
and this gardener
dead in the heat of midday.

♪

Bird Watcher

Having lost his footing at an early age
he was stranded in the branches of a city.
He watched the words he could not communicate
fly away in cloud formation.

Separated from himself
he stared at space. Scorning machines.
He longed to part the banks of cloud drift
to rise and fall in shafts of air.
As his bones became heavier
so the desire to fly became greater.

After years of practice, he found
that by walking slowly, his feet
lifted him a short distance from the ground
continuing their walking movement until he was airborne.

Cautious, he never attempted this unless
in the right frame of mind.

As he became more experienced
he found it easy to lie in the air horizontally.
Wiser, he no longer tried to fly after the unobtainable.
Disentangling himself from his leafless embrace

he is flying into the silence where
he contains his body.

♪

Farmer's Fantasy

'It were from a black toad,
with a star on its back
found under an owd felled log,'
his grandfather whispering before he died,
thrusting it into his hand.

And it worked.
Horses obeyed him,
the cow's milk was richer,
crops never failed,
no warts in the family.
Power at his finger-tips.
Nothing deceived him.

The tiny thing in his pocket
little black bone
smooth, polished, a fearful inheritance.

If the snow could blanket his thoughts
gently freeze his brain,
cover the furniture that walked in the night
that stood by his bed
in response to his dreams.

Nowhere was safe.
Still he fingered the bone in his pocket,
afraid to think.
Afraid to let go.

'When the snow melts
when the mist rises
when summer comes
when harvest's done
at the next pheasant's call
or the first thunder storm.
Then. Then I'll bury it.'

But he couldn't stop thinking.

'I must fetch me a spade from the barn,'
as he left the house,
the spade coming to meet him
you could almost say walking.

♪

Letter to Christopher

Greetings from the land of make-believe!
Raise your glass
let's drink to life!
It will surprise everyone.

Afternoon of another day
we walk through gates, through fields
the sky rising and dipping
calling: Look! No clouds!
Today – wind, rain.
Leaves tumble bright colours
the swallows gone
mulberries over.
Do you understand the man alone
boxing, whispering insults to his shadow?
The man alone, running

beating time
while two women holding peacock feathers
stare at each other?
Learning has just slipped past –
did you see?
My hands fill with air, fingers swell like sausages,
my head with dried twigs.
What you said was evil is only life –
but treat it with care
watch out for the sting in its tail.

How the rain beats down on the garden chairs.
What matters now is the revolving
of the word-wheel.
Cocooned, marooned in pockets of sun and mist
we live our future in our palms
and float bodiless in night
becoming the words we thought.
Friend, dear friend, did you know
that the wide open spaces
are the gaps in God's mouth?

♪

When You Come into Your Country

To come out of
be released from
covers a new time

Precariously
listening for your approach
I am breathless after
the first few steps

Tree felled
wood splinters
true
A true splinter?
Breathless
absurd
with a splinter in my back
and the borrowed crown
listening, expecting you hourly

The birds have a new time
in the changing moon
The cows on the hill top
are warriors not animals
and your country is rolling distant

The tree inside me
splinters when I fall
often
with love divorced from love

Remember
let the burning be brief
not in vain
not consuming
when you
come into
your kingdom

February 14th

The sea
swallows the pebbles
throws them up
Afternoon passed
Sun intermittent

To want nothing
to be content with nothing
Needs grow not lessen
Meaning vanishes from time to time
Acts of kindness may be suspect

Heart-beat
bird cry
mist
brooding marsh

Railings growing out of the mind
lapped by mist
revealing a spire
and the sea another drumming

Words of love in a foreign language
sea
mist
to send messages through
to penetrate
heaviness
Mind encroaching
fields
lapped by waves
evening comes with snow

Light in a window
The room glowing in the trees
where the lamps hang in winter air

Returning
through obsequious mist
giving back
And how should it be otherwise?

Only without need is love
Age-old gestures of tenderness
and the words of love again and again
carried on the wind

Nothingness is impossible

Illumined
justified
to walk in filled space
enfolded, separate

Not to give
give back
receive

And I have come
hurried, distracted
having done nothing without difficulty

Touching the floor
mute
unable to comprehend the light

Elusive Love Poem

Master of disguises
you appear in the most unexpected places –
platforms of railway stations
deep footprints in snow drifts
on an icy wind from the East
or at polite dinner parties when
conversation is tiring.
Now, once again, you are near
as I sit in a dirty train
which carries me out of a past I'm unwilling to leave
leading me where I would not go.

Travelling since first light
from North to South
exchanging pleasantries en route
with a travelling juggler and
a musician from Rome.
All passengers pale and anxious.
The effects of a hard winter?
Industrial turmoil?
We are sceptical pilgrims
knowing well that the world has not
promised anything to anybody.

Your hand presses my heart –
the falcon does not struggle when caught.
Your words are always with me.
One day I will sing unrestricted.

Boundaries

Your hard
palm upwards
the untranslatable mist –
I cannot touch you
but I walk towards you
blow you aside
lift you lovingly
through unopened windows

You know how nothing matters but the stones
solitary, circling
and the moment which never passes

It always comes back to this –
after the fling into darkness –
this sun on the grass circle
and a wish for silence

♪

Truth Unveiled

The spring of Time
has dried up
and in the middle of the circle
is a speck of dust

Songs a Thracian Taught Me

The Thracians lamented birth because of the hard life which awaited the newly born. They rejoiced at death and believed they could communicate with the gods. Every five years they chose by lot one among them to send as emissary to Zaimoxis to tell him of their needs. They sent the messenger thus: several soldiers seized him by the arms and legs, several other soldiers stood with spears upright, the messenger was rocked in the air and cast upon the spears. If he died the god was favourable to them. If he lived the messenger was considered an evil man and another messenger was chosen.

They played a game akin to Russian roulette: a warrior stood on a stone with his head through a hangman's noose, holding in his hand his sword. The stone would be kicked away and the game was to cut the rope before it tightened round his neck. Sometimes he was not quick enough and died. The onlookers thought this extremely amusing.

Birth

Put on the mask
the lips perfect
the eyes hollow

This is the hard time
And the metal must be beaten
into a shape which weeps

Communication

To memorise
words
to be sent
by messenger

to a place
no messenger living
could be sent

To dispatch
a messenger
on spears –
skilfully welded –
held high
for the messenger
to float down on
onwards to another city

To tell the departed
the words
memorised
to describe how
painful
the struggle
to place the feet
on the path
of the living

Love Song of the Thracian Horseman

I will throw you
only the chicken breast
and the largest crusts
from the whitest bread

You shall drink the best
wine from my cup
your lips on
the imprint of mine

I will give you
seventeen gold beads
each one a flower
on a gold chain

I will give you
some bracelets
yellow snakes to coil
lovingly over your arms

I will hand you
my sharpest spear
that you may impale me
on our love

You are my wild
golden-maned horse
I shall gallop you
miles into the night

Roulette

Destiny is
a tightening rope
swinging between
air and air

Psalm of Death

Rejoice dearly beloved
we are gathered together
in the passage of time

to become jewels
wrought on a living scythe

The Gift

Speak now
of the golden horses
swifter
than the wind –
beautiful
the sound of their hooves
on
the ever-changing ridge of light

Gold
captured in the light
of
changing winds –
uncontrollable
plunging of fierce breath
no hand
trembling can hold
such power

God's Country

The Anglo-Saxon inhabitants of East Anglia, descendants of the Teutonic tribes from Europe, were converted to Christianity in the two decades that followed the setting-up of a bishopric at Dunwich in 630. The first bishop was Felix, a Burgundian who had been ordained bishop in Gaul. In the centuries that followed so many abbeys and churches were built in Suffolk, the southern half of East Anglia, that in time it became known as Silly Suffolk, the word 'silly' being derived from the Saxon *saelig* meaning holy or blessed. Today in the coastal belt from Southwold to Sutton Hoo one occasionally hears older residents speak about God's Country. It is an area of many moods, grey-blue sea, white-tipped waves, ribbons of fine hard sand, shifting shingle shining in the sunlight, flat desolate marshes and barren gorse-covered heathland. Almut was an Anglo-Saxon woman of Germanic descent who lived there.

1

The unfolding of the earth
the ploughing

sea birds in brown
rising and falling

stretches on towards
heath, heather, broom

finally sea
battering sandy cliffs

Long dreamt-of snowdrops
to be sung

by the gentler winds

and it is full turning again

never varying
neither shadow of turning

stiff limbs relax
in the sun's warming

Walking to villages
sounding strangely
contemplation of future
of now
and the buds' bursting

I speak for the women

moods uncertain and restless rain
doubly I live
waiting
a condition of living

And I walk, tired, in the changeable winds
cold, sometimes, singing, singing
for a love to be lightly held

Old woman, I said,
where is your wisdom?

She spread her hands
'In the bones, my love,
in the toughened skin
my hands have touched and
tended all things

In the groaning breath —
do you come near to hear it?
time was when my lungs
filled the moors with laughing —

but in my black skirt and bent back
you'll find no solutions
No, go your way
and I'll go mine
the old one in her days
will not hesitate to ask the babe
about the pace of life
it's the years have wings'

Moving always more slowly
on two sticks
she goes before me to sleep abroad

The snow flickers on newly built nests

2

The black dog lopes by my side.
He has taken to following me,
and we find fossils and shells
up here on the wooded heath
where adders bask when there's sun.

Neighbours are afraid of the dog –
not an animal, they say, half human.
Has been seen for nigh on a hundred years,
the devil's pet, they say, be on guard –
a boy was lured into the sea
by a wild, dark man who barked
and yelped as he dragged him down.

Well, dog or no dog
when the mist is over the dead grass
and the owl cries from the willow tree
when the gaunt giants, standing sentry

to the farm, wink as I pass
I pat the rough coat and feel comforted.

The women weave closer
their colours immediate.
Not to mind
the cooking, cleaning
the chatter, nagging,
the scoldings of husband, of children,
which sums up the being of women.

What is happening?
Where are the promises?
The east wind slashes your cheeks
mighty warrior cleaving your skulls
leaving no bruises or blood.
Yet you bleed to death.
How many times will you turn in your grave?

The sea claims the land
fierce is the long fading
bitter the waves

When the bones scream
under the power
colours darken
skies darken

There are men who have power
who control others with a look, a gesture

The tree of knowledge just out of reach
black wings carry their words on the swell of the waves

Time is infirmity
Turn aside, let the air heal
I look towards nothing for a second sight

3

We are restless when the wind
blows up from the North,
lashing the almond blossom into the well,
nudging the nesting blackbird,
stirring our latent hatreds –
although we live together calmly,
very tranquil in the dying storms,
attuned more to the elements than to each other.

Be wary of the women shivering
on the marsh at high tide –
they have planted oats and barley
helped their husbands chop the wood,
obeyed in every way.
They turn to face their partners.
The rings are lost, the circle broken.

Good 'bor, let me gather the coneys from your trees,
walk on your village green unmolested.
All that is mine belongs likewise to you.
The limbs tire
the spirit flags.
He who has money can eat sherbet in Hell.

I will tell of the pure voices
and the bells pealing under the sea
for those who want to hear them.
You shall have some joy in knowing
the futility of all things.

Let me dig up the roots of love
to replant them here
where the walls crumble
where no one walks
where wild roses twine round the ancient cross
and the sound from the sea is only a murmur —
in peace let it flourish.
Take my hand, joy is the slow dance
which I must learn in good time.

4

Dawn is early in July
the cock crows at three.
I watch the night recede
and listen for the barley bird.
More than enough in the coming day.

Always a new charm
be it a ring with a lucky stone
or a scarf of the prescribed colour
according to the sun.

The magic doesn't work.

I call you thoughtfully.
No response.

I'm like a somnambulist who suffers from insomnia.

Down the lane the honeysuckle grows in the hedge.
I say aloud: Is it possible to be in two places at once?

And after the silence
falling

after the mist clears
face down on the marshy grass
rubbed out
far out
past bones, past juniper trees
tasting the mud
exposed to the ridicule
cut by the whip
I see you
blood of my blood,
and put the honeysuckle in your hand.

Listen. The wind sweeps laughing over
the bewitched land.
A few red petals fall –
there's been no rain for weeks.

The sheep have gone mad,
the ghosts of two white horses
chase them round the oak tree
round and round – their bleating
a melancholy echo.

Not wanting to cheat your world
not wanting to run away
I take a walk at recreation time
to recreate my shrinking world.

These are the bones that did not live
died darker than the sand which covered them.
These are the bones alive three hundred years ago
with no thought of the distance.

And I have learnt to sit on an upright chair
talking with the women of childbirth,
preserving fruit and the price of wool.

5

The sun breaks mist
revealing summer trees
and cows stilled in greyness.

Warmth and mystery surround this place today.
So much might happen.
Let us make three tents in the garden –
and wait.
The moods come up and down
as gently as the butterfly swings on the buddleia.

If I should meet you,
down the lane
or at the waves breaking,
face to face in the world turned golden,
seagulls mewing somewhere there over the hedge,
your open hand
would hold my sinking.

6

The wind rattled my sleep
shook me awake in the early hours:
Uncover the crumbling walls
uncover the vine
unlock your heart
leave no key unturned
this pain must out
out of depth
out of sight
out of mind.

The aching body of the house,
where horse bones ward off the Evil Eye,
creaked and groaned in the ebbing tide.

These are the days of ripening pears
and harvesting late into the evening.
Mulberry days
the mist thick on water as moon fades
sun rises.

Marigolds grow by the kitchen door
or in pots on the window sills –
a wise woman once told me: 'Plant a marigold
in the soil from your love's footprint
these flowers will never fade
neither will his love.'

The young women walk alone on the shingle
where river swirls and circles into the sea.
They look out from isolated windows
across brown stones towards grey water.
Women with names to hide
names hidden in pots of marigolds
in hag-stones under the pillows.

I grow weary
watch others grow weary.
Watch heartaches, disappointments
transform into heart pains and rheumatism.
If you would keep your love
fix a nail in his footprint
soothe him with camomile –
then wash his shirts.

Charm with Stones

Walking the cliff path
to the edge of the precipice
to the edge of the precipice
where river and sea boil together
over myriads of stones
over myriads of stones
leaving nothing unheard
leaving nothing
but sound
under gorse and wild desolation

It's you
you
I was looking for
on this still day of strange sun
and to find you here
at the end of the path
where the sand falls
on cornelians and agates
shining in waters fresh and salt

and the light dimming
or brightening
according to time
the branches of cherry trees
with blossom or red leaves
according to time.
I have found you and lost you
according to time
from dreams to uninspired days

back to dreams

where you frown or smile
waking me to walk the cliff path
walk the sand
the cornelians and agates
in strange sun
over myriads of unheard stones

My love is like a red red rowan berry
promising renewed life
I close the gates

No, not to keep you out
to keep you in
to seal you from prying fingers
to lock you against the wind

Vespers

All day the sun
on fallen leaves from the mulberry tree
magic circle of yellow leaves
in a day of frosty sun.
For everyone there is the time for loving
to everything there is a purpose.

So the day has passed
with the curlew's sad cry
and the warm hissing of the stove.
A shape brushes the window
is it a leaf or a bat?

I bring before you this room
candle-lit, peaceful now,
and this love,
grown painfully
to hold the pheasants shining
the changing autumn winter land
and all unspoken passions,
bring them to you
in circles of flame around each face
softer light from the blue glass on blue curtains
under shadow of wings
where there is time for time.

Encounter

To wish someone 'the sele of the morning' is a Suffolk greeting –
meaning to wish them well.

I gave the sele of the morning
to the man breaking stones
by the wayside

Where does this road lead?
I asked,
to the hills?

So it does,
he replied.
Unseen someone passed
between the pear and the yew tree
a bird flew up
in sudden fright

All day strange figures
came and went
all day

I picked stones
from the wayside
dreaming of hills

Night came
morning came
houses crumbled in the heat

Do you go up the road,
said the man,
and keep walking

King Solomon and the Cuckoo

The daily provisions for Solomon were thirty measures of fine flour and thirty measures of meal, ten fatted oxen, twenty free-grazing oxen, one hundred sheep, besides deer and gazelles, roebucks and fatted cuckoos. – I KINGS

Many a spring evening
I walked in the gardens of Sheba's joy –
'Why do you smile, O King may you live forever?
In your wisdom answer me.'
There began my rotting bird of no worth,
there began the lie.
'Thou art fair, beloved,
thou, too, art wise. Know this –
that even in laughter the heart finds sadness.'

Clear and thrilling your song, unworthy carrion,
you saw through those fine words,
the enthralling discussion. You know
that the king, who will not live for ever,
thought that a hand in a hand was worth two hundred
in a harem – therefore he smiled –
at his own wit.

As the riches piled up
so you probed my heart.
As I sat on the great ivory throne
with sun on pure gold
year after year people came marvelling, questioning,
yours was the voice with a sceptic note.

Food in abundance –
but I take no pleasure in oxen or sheep,
have no taste for deer.

My mouth waters for your delectable flesh.

I've had you fattened
forced meal down your throat
and rejoiced when you appeared on a golden platter
smothered in onions.

What do you know of love, excruciating songbird?
You, who scatter your offspring from nest to nest.
Fat, ugly babies making room for themselves
by stealthy killing, while you watch unobserved
bewitching us all with your song
which inspires mawkish music.
From the land of my dreams
I hear you.

In the courtyards of precious stones,
on the pillars of almuggin wood
I see you,
bird of no particular beauty,
laughing, mocking me as though you had
knowledge of my end.

Backward Glance

A crown of thorns
over the loving bed –
not a question of reliving,
more a groping,
a quest for the Holy Grail –
tentative as a bird's flight
down narrow stairs
further
deeper ...
this was no ordinary thing.

Ducks paddling in mud
round a small island
where corpse and corpse embrace.
In dim winter light
a cart, a bell and a cry:
Rag and Bone!

He stood in the market place
shouting to all who passed:
I have living bread!

and indeed you could see it breathe
under his hands

while passers-by
walked into dreams
buying pomegranates instead of apples
breathless with the daring of it.

The Mill Owner's Wife

A Victorian Story

He brought me – here.
Built this grey house
dug me a garden fenced in
with black railings.

He employed a gardener
to plant, cultivate:
'For my wife, my love,
she likes flowers, strawberries –
grow them and more.'

And how could this cold place
grow sunshine
or colour?

He took me to stroll
in the evenings
along a flagged path
to the terrace.
We looked at the hills and the valley
of chimneys, factories
floating in smoke.
I heard a bell from the church
chime without joy.

'What else, my love,
can I do for your happiness?
Aren't you pleased
with the garden
the magnificent view?'

He built a stone bench
in the shelter of brick
ordered silk cushions
soft rugs for my comfort.
On fine days I sat
and sat there.

I longed for the sun
on white-washed cottages
for the clear sea of deep light.
I saw donkeys burdened
with olives, led by women
up steep cobbled steps.

There are logs piled on the fire
in this hushed room where
he hardly dare tread –
he turns away sighing –

I hate and pity the love
which he gave.

Nothing left – here –
but rain overflowing the streams
and wind gusting on moors
towards uncheerful crags.

Obsession

... but always when he turned away from her into himself he left her holding Nothing in her hands and staring at it, calling it many names but knowing it was only the hope that he would come back soon. —

F. SCOTT FITZGERALD, *Tender is the Night*

I'll not give you away
to some earnest minister
nor let them burn you with the tip of a flower
You hold me with your eyes
your voice
your very mouth keeps me near

Shake me off if you dare
I have gone mad it seems
and time alone with you
is sad paradise
No one knows my absence
or the places where I find you
where we lie under shadows

I search for you in my dreams
never daring to mention your name
never describing you
even to myself

Part of you
part of me
twined tight
ivy, convolvulus

When I curse at the helplessness
and horror
it is your devotion calms the world

and you are Colossus tearing apart
the rocks, sea
You toss them away
they float high, higher
all shapes, colours, gleaming
fragments of my brain

I have gone mad
but no one knows
A secret you keep locked
the key thrown into the abyss

You have gathered cool herbs
and your cooler hands
stroke my head gently, gently
in the afternoon

The Question

He looked up
his book still in his hand,
that dazed expression
so well known
saddened her.

But, he did look up,
looked through her
out to the window,
garden, robin perched
on japonica – briefly.

She spoke into the void
of his mind – or hers
'Not again, never.'
Nothing moved
even outside nothing stirred.

'Understand I can't
explain it more.'
Again the silent afternoon
the fear on her neck.

And slowly she watched
his eyes move slowly back
the book trembling – briefly –
in the heat.

Survival

It wasn't clear
whether the patient spoke
or the body
shifted an arm
to brush away a fly

The doctor
roused from
an infrequent embrace
swore it was none of his doing

Into the mind of the corpse
entered a sensation
of buzzing

untenable
when one hopes to lie
peacefully

and then being lifted
drawn forth
not to be described in English
moved him to utter
a word or two

hardly a complaint
even in his extremity
he remembered
biting the hand that feeds

and later
in the train

with his granddaughter
he repeated the Russian
for dying
indicating a corner of dirty window
where a fly
tried to get out

♪

Brook Farm in June

The pond
the garden.
Washing line between apple trees.
Table
chairs by an open window.
From this window
the child with floury hands
sugar on her nose
smiles a welcome.
There
see in the far meadow
those hooded figures
working –
they will come home when the bell rings out
summoning them for tea and bread.
Farmers have found relics of forgotten saints.

Three floors under the dairy
great flagstones – peace uncovered.

We drink wine
listen to sonatas played on a tinkly piano –
warmth and honeysuckle everywhere.

Despair stands aside
prayer is the answer
in this house
where a baby is soon to be born
in the upstairs room.

Despair stands aside
we shall not die but live and declare
that the sky is a flight route for herons
children will ring the Angelus
and drift to sleep with voices at Compline
while wheat grows taller
and partridges run red-legged
between the fields.

Letters to Constantine

1

Today I begin with nothing
imagine a dog
worrying at a bone of nothingness.
Think of the space nothing takes up.

Torn between nothing and nothing
the house cast in outer darkness
where mice act as spies
and discreet spiders spin webs
thicker and thicker
securing doors, windows,
while vampire bats
beat their wings in the attic
to frighten off loving marauders
who take nothing.

Mealy mouthed existence of nothingness
to be able to do it so well
with such grace –
oh God, give me strength to continue doing it
if I must.

2

Some women
are left washing up at weddings
when the family
holding the champagne glasses
pose for the festival photograph.

Dizzy, tired out
by the noise
of over-excited children
they stand at unfamiliar sinks
and dream of space craft

arriving on the lawn
filling the garden with silent music
exotic flowers and gentle shadows.

Shadows of dreams only
for these women also know
the outcome of weddings ...
later, at home they remove
their straw hats
and veil their eyes.

3

From the window see
the people hurry across the square
a bell chimes
evening.
Have you considered
the significance of squares?
I have circled them often
at different times
all memorable.

Tonight, memories are swollen
no one to ease the pain
which drifts constantly.

Your image has faded
mine is tarnished –

a sadness brought on by daffodils
and ripening seed.

There is a saying:
'If the cherry blossom
falls into the jam
swallows leave early.'

But why do I speak of Spring
when the longest day
has passed in a shower of rain?

4

Late September
Boston –
shines through my jumbled mind
like the sun
in Fenway Park
I took your arm
and we strolled
among the roses –
lingered there
talking of religion –
And I can clearly see
the parked car we passed
that Sunday morning

a man dead
in the driver's seat.

5

Life has to do with passing –
having no permanence –
there are many ways
at times almost a giving
It is said
that sorrow passes –
happiness does.
People pass out of your life
living
and leave you
dying.

6

Last night
the storm tried to break in
it howled through the ash tree
broke the window latch
I was blinded and afraid.

The sun blew away
the moon blew away
the sea threw up its dead
without glory.

My hand shakes even now
as I listen to the children
on their way to school
and watch the words on the page
melt with laughing.

I send you my love
since that does not depend on time.

7

Enclosed is the first autumn leaf
from the ornamental cherry tree
first in the garden to redden and fall.

Night has left behind strange powers –
disturbed, something inside me is crying.
Sun shines on the yellow daisies
pears drop from the old tree
and the wind is gentle.
Whose shadow on my door?
Who spoke my name?

The children have been here.
Small sticky fingers have caressed my face
small legs and arms clung to my body –
all heaving earth to remind of loss and gain.

It grieves me as I watch
the mulberries ripen
that year after year we never meet.

Once, a magpie flew across our path
you were angry because I would not wait:
'One for sorrow,' you said
but I was always in a hurry
being sceptical of two for joy.

Today I would wait –
I imagine standing with you
by the hawthorn, fingers linked
silent, almost breathless with watching for
the sweeping wings
and seeing all our life spread out across the fields.
Was it you who passed?

You who spoke?
Or do you lie under some heavy stone
and no one to tell me?

Mothers, Daughters, Mothers

Demeter speaks from her cave:
But let me in accord with the times
become thoughtful.
All the more so to analyse my conflicts.
I have searched the unspoken.
No longer turn men into owls
or attempt the impossibilities of immortality.
And if it were so
we would not want a reliving.
For one reason or another
our bones are close knit.
The seeds of the pomegranate
flourish in a transparent setting.
With armfuls of wheat and roses
already withering
I stand neither here nor there
knowing that the living must not look back.

And Persephone replies from Hades:
We have shared the seeds from the pomegranate
and I have described the mists over the river
the sharp rocks, cold to the touch
hardly seen ...
we have explored the domain I rule.
To hope in the future is out of place
to hope in the past is out of time.
Over and over again I will refill your arms
... living or dying we cross the same fields.

Cul-de-Sac

He switched off the television
lit a cigarette
walked to the window.

He could hear his wife
talk to herself
softly
downstairs, just below
where he stood by the open window.

'Troops on the border,
manoeuvres ...'
always at this time of year
a sort of army holiday
with room to expand,
'No invasion as yet.'

Time off from work
to calm his nerves
except that the news on TV
was driving him crazy with fear
and his dear wife
talking alone in the kitchen
increased his frenzy
except that his stiff upper lip
was hardened to iron.

She switched off the television
sick of stage directions,
the lighting of cigarettes,
pouring of drinks,
slamming of car doors

by unreal characters
toying with violence
or social problems –
plays meant to distract her
from remembering missiles
hidden in forests nearby ...

She was meant to forget
the unreal characters
selling missiles
to unreal characters
who set up frontiers
to keep troops on the borders
who build shelves
for stacking the dead.

They switched off the television
put the cat out
put the baby to bed
finishing the whisky they opened
the pineapple juice
found brown paper bags and
two suitcases –
prepared to exit
right or left
according to stage directions.

Resurrection

Very early
          daybreak
a slight stirring
          faint

because rain poured down
      and all awash

The stone was
      still in place
no light
no sound

A voice in my head
      whispered appropriate words
but my tongue was imprisoned

People who live
      in the shadow of the great
have had
      their reward

♪

The 'Good' Man Montségur

Circa 1242-3

That was a stronghold worth remembering
slung high on a sheer cliff
the walls hewn from rock face.

And the view –
heavenly when the sun shone –
miles and miles of it.

What abounded in those walls was love
the kind that's
hardly fashionable now.

Music, too, drifting down into the valley
even when snow covered our world.
Our world was small
not safe, but warm
deeply peaceful in spite of
what can only be described as danger.

And it is not the smoke
nor the burning
I wish to remember

only the rough pasture where
our goats fed, their bells
mournful on summer evenings,

only the boulders and rocks
haphazard, watchfully eerie
where turquoise lizards hid

where ravens perched.
Consolation lived
around and about us.

Fear too? Perhaps a quiver
for this husk's last pain
but think if you please

of the release from servitude
the weary treadmill
of our endless births.

Look again. Hear again.
Bend down and scoop a handful of earth
feel how it crumbles.

Many Christmases

Rusty gold of dead bracken
burning wood wafts incense over the roof
myrrh I have none.

Slight confusion as to place
but room or stable available –
no caves in this area.

Shepherds, kings, angels
all could be found
and there are stars in plenty.

But where is the Child?
I search through layers of wrapping
and through icy rooms
where the little ones are locked
to hide bruises and burns.
Many others dimly glimpsed
spindle-legged, whimpering
with infected eyes and
swollen bellies.

Behind the raised glasses
beneath the tinsel I peer
groping in darkness –
for the light of this season
is evasive.

The Fallow Land

People climb high places to weep
for the smoke drifts
east, west, east
the sea roars far off –
as yet nothing happens.

I listen to the rain outside
hear the hum from the radiator
it's warm enough, snug is the word.
Light falls on us both.

'What's beyond?' you ask.
The garden, of course
wilder now, a haven for wild ones.
'And beyond?'
Oh, the village,
church clock chimes the hour,
pub, gossip in the shop.

You look, you want to see further
further where the straight white road
leads out and away.
Rain, steam, blot out the view
my mind is dimmer.
This mistake is to look for happiness
it comes and goes
as the long-tailed tit swaying
on the emptying pear tree –
I tried to hold it
and now tell the same old lies
which are half believed in the same old way.

Not even through my eyes
will you see the spray of autumn leaves –
seven, deeply red against
the tangle of buddleia.

No words reach you
no raindrops touch you
you have taken the white road
turned aside to the fallow land
and it is permitted to weep
while learning to count by years not days.

In Memoriam

Edward Packer

She stripped the sheets from your bed
and lay sleepless
in the blank night
fingers grasping tightly
on her own hand.

Now the fog
freezes into the bones
and you are shrouded
out there
somewhere
perhaps smiling
as the sun
slowly breathes on the white land
to clear the air.

Now the snow

frozen on the little streams
in new-found woods
forms a layer of ice in my heart
which will not melt
which will not
let you leave this place
where you are joking
and your eyes ask questions.

Now in the village
is a gap –
a quick passing –
shops lack requirements
lanes are impassable
flooded
and your voice
wordless in my ear.

Well, it is fanciful
as you must know –
black-veiled women with shaking hands
sort out your small belongings
you cannot be replaced when spring comes
like rotting doors or windows
and she will mourn you
long after summer
sadly
without fuss
the unmown grass
a reminder of your space.

The Art of Memory

Write down the rain
the inner hollowness of winter light
on cold earth

Place the notes
of your unfinished symphony in a box
labelled 'might have been'

Write down the bridge
shadows on curling water
or trees heavy with summer leaf

In the church lamps are lit
flicker under serene faces
and through the quietness
voices sing out a fading day

My head suddenly
holds the universe
cloud on cloud of not knowing

Lift up that most unjoyful heart
and cry out thanks
into the freshening wind
where forked branches
are landmarks of an all-seeing eye

Brook Farm, Easter 1982

The door bangs
a hem of blue wool
blows over the cracks in the floor.

Sun setting almost unnoticed.
Family gather for supper,
child asleep with arms round a chocolate egg.

There was no speaking in tongues
in this farmhouse
with daffodils walking down
the flagstone passage
only the wind murmurs sullenly
at the pigs' swill.

The Spring smells harsh.

What language have we left
to tell of hours
which remain unpassing?
Taste
smell
sight
heightened till death bangs a door
on the hem of blue wool
and the tiny flames flicker
just out of sight.

Everything still now
no pigs
no carts
fields stretch out

the path falters on stones
come from nowhere
a night without stars.

♪

Meeting

She expected a caress –
standing miles away
at a railway station
somehow unreal
with snow and steam engines
weirdly silent for so large a town

Had she been waiting
for someone in particular
no one came

Perhaps it was the wrong station
should have been further south
heat rising with foreign perfume
brim of a hat shading her eyes

Surprised when asked
for an ash-tray
with a look more of anger
than love

Her voice
reminded her of iron heels
on the platform
as the over-crowded train pulled away
and the room
growing colder

with chairs well apart
each to his own thought

♪

Four Poems from the Chinese

1

Last pale clouds of sunset
calm the approaching night.

A small breeze brushes aside the falling curtain
remaining sun fades into the blue trees.

Gradually pointed light blots out the window
and the garden sighs in brief desolation.

Autumn breathes coldly on the pool
ruffling opaque images in its green depth.

If he could share his love
together they might pluck the strings of understanding.

2

In the golden wine of Autumn
dew is suddenly morning frost.

Pliant branches stiffen between dawn and sunset
green leaves turn yellow between day and night.

The moon emerges behind cloud cliffs

bright the skein of pure light.

At daybreak from the balcony I see wild geese
fly up with hungry cries.

Ambition covers the four seas
but solitary I prefer the empty courtyard.

3

Imagine the summit of Mount Wu
dusk falling on its crooked terraces.

Misty clouds swiftly unfurl, refurl
monkeys and birds now and again are silent.

As if such beauty could be anticipated
confused words break off as you gaze.

Wistfully we sit below the green courtyard
longing for the Autumn wind.

4

Mountains between the approaching mists
bamboo amid a glimpse of sun
birds fly towards the eaves

from the window clouds pass.

Moving a Church

No one about
but me
watching
the fat one
the thin one

two unlikely
out-of-date men
as though carrying Christ
to the holocaust
what was she doing
with an aching heart
losing the thread

the icon tipped
unsteadily
through the church door?

'Those priests
with greasy
hair'
she said
'to have believed ...'

'What was given
is taken'
I said
and to dream
that you dreamt of death
is a sign of good luck

Not that she heard me

rain in London
on Saturday
is not conducive to listening

♪

A Place in the Sun

At last she frightened a part of herself –
all airy fairy in blue-ribboned dress –
free to go where she pleased
when she pleased,
weakly protesting:
'Don't judge by appearances
his face would be nice if he were happier,'
nursing her bruised arm
as he held up his hand to show her
the missing finger:
'Do you think I could be cruel
after such a misfortune?'
His eyes bright with malice.

Every move she made he foresaw
every place she went he was before her –
to take over, live through her, in her
was what he intended.

She cried for help for that part of her
darkened and hardened
which he had struck.

'My head,' he said, 'your heart,
my hand
your finger
part of a part that has nothing to offer

165

but with patience I will grow.'
Escape to the sun
get away from it all
relax on warm sands
extra wine to blot out his presence
which lingers
spreads in her voice
bursting through their sky
exposing her cruelty
his pain.

♪

Two Exercises for the Left Hand

1

These were my waiting thoughts –
not for me the tearing heat
the cooling song
not for me the everlasting sweat
of work half finished half begun.
But you
oh, you came through
smiling
perfect
to take applause
without a word
a murmur of the truth.

These were my waiting thoughts
so full of anger and despair
my very life hung in the balance –
but you
oh, you came through

came through my half-forgotten sleep
'Don't cry,'
you said,
'there are many others
much worse off
and sin'
yes, sin is what you called it,
'drains your strength.'

These were my waiting thoughts
for me the unfulfilled
for you the gain
you came between myself and me
had twisted all my words,
stolen the sweet breath of thought
to take these passionate horses
all fire and flowing manes
their feet on newly growing turf –
the bed of life – of death.

2

This is no pretence
no place not sunk deep
embedded, as they say, in flesh.
It overflows
seeps
even at table
it floods the eyes till plate and fork
obscured
hand fumbles.

Riding in
near the root
which nears the rot

stabbing at membrane
or is it my own nails
tearing at the splintered dark

Lulled by kisses
betrayed by calm
shaken by storm

From the depths
from the depth, as they say,
the voice hardly human.

Images

Holding up her child
to see the birds
she said:
'Everything means something to you –
even a feather fallen on the rosemary –
and you are right to smile and clap.'

Not for this
answered his eyes
reflecting the vines
on the cut-out hills –
grapes not yet formed.

'Do you hear them chirp?'
she asked, putting him from her
ready to catch him lest he fall
'and the wind in the pines?
The far-away sea?'

Not for this
answered the clay birds
stretching their wings
turning to flesh at his approach.

'What I am saying,'
the woman said, pulling him gently
from the bank of the stream
where he played with stones and moss
changing the water's course,
'this garden is a work of art
painted on wood.
Between my mind and the future dream
is desert
our tears the memorable oasis.'

♪

Poem for Greta

She sat sewing
tea-cups on the table
windows open
Why is it I mention
the years between us?

Her presence hovers
her eyes shining, shining
I look for Spring

A long way we've come
to be lullabied
in a garden of dreams

Behind the trees horses

yes still there my dear,
they'll come for me in time

If your eyes
could have spoken sooner
in my mouth
we would have sat – so –
with tea-cups and mending

We have changed places
your voice fades
and my hands touch air

♪

A Kind of Homage to Chekhov

Those sisters
always wanting what they couldn't have –
not seagulls, not actresses ...
what is it about them comes to mind
in the branches of the sleeping beech tree?

Acceptance, perhaps, albeit grudged,
of a changing life which stretches
on and on
when all the cherry orchards have been felled.

Their father looks at us
with a sad sympathy:
'I created you,' he says,
'who swore to live, who smile or weep
as the world falls apart.'

Across the sky wild geese cackle,

snow melts, snowdrops push themselves
towards the light.
'When Spring comes,' we murmur,
almost trusting the February sun.

♪

When Reporting a Missing Person

You wonder why
nothing was done
no move made to discover
his strange vanishing ...

when he went to fetch wood
nothing happened in my mind.
Night rolled where trees and sky meet
owls hooted beyond the garden fence
I sat in a cold kitchen

Dawn came
blackbirds begged for food
peewits ventured near the door
there was a dead weasel by the wall

Stepping into a frosty garden
I found no trace –
fragments of sunlight
splintered in my dull brain
silence hung from every twig ...

so you understand
everything comes to him who waits

Snowbound Journey

To Hans Arp

Now fear has abandoned the greater part of men
and infinity hasn't one kind word,
one fearful word to say them.
Yawning voids grow next to yawning voids.
                                    — JEAN HANS ARP

It is required to die —
to find oneself the main principle
of the journey,
to accept for the first time
the entering alone ...
assembling in profound silence
a motionless relationship ...

and this dying
on condition
never again to be excited with nothing
or sit before an empty cup,
absent minded, ashamed.

People will probably disperse
inspired with peculiar tongue,
concealing sly smiles
walk out through strange doorways,
their ambassador laying the last card
on the table.
And surrounded
for a hundred years
in wastes of marsh and ice
you will overshadow
your image of a slender heart.

With difficulty
glide against time
unresponsive, mute

having learnt,
one way or another,
to be beside yourself.

♪

Cold Spell

All kinds of shapes
to be surprised by
notice
snow on early almond blossom

exceedingly solitary
the fields now
all is motionless

to right and left
are Japanese pictures
and pale lamplight in the farm window

worlds beyond worlds
we are so far removed

when we awake

The Argument

Let go my throat
you win
I'm thrown off balance
your beauty has me on my knees.

But which of us is cruel?
You know it all.
Oh, yes, my name is Legion
that I can't deny
but you planned it all – not me –
everything miraculous
in the end it's more like mockery.

Let me examine
your transparency
your deceit – no, truth I mean –
let me give you my account
of all that happened in these long years.

It's not the first time I've been at fault
but you tell me about the circling game
of age on age
the torn branch, the endless munching
of blood and bits of bone.
Your clean perfection
against my filth.

So many shapes have visited my door
so many images crossed my mind
when leaves die patiently
and love and love again has tied my hands.
Whose choice was that?

Comfort?
None
not now
your silence zooming in my head
nothing left but everything
even the breath I take
belongs to you.

♪

Beginnings and Endings

When the gods
were led into the world
the lonely
stayed in darkness
waiting for the dawn to crow

The gods fled heavenwards
filling the air with joyful explosions
and showers of many-coloured sparks

As sunlight penetrated the gloom
the lonely found themselves
and quiet
with light step
they walked across the lawn

Scattered among the rosebushes
and clumps of stocks
were the burnt-out gods

Tenderly
the lonely
carried them home

♪

Protest

Since Tuesday
I have wept
from head to foot
from morning to night

This is the moment
for truth and clarity
if not in words
or music
then I'll take a brush
and slash paint across the wall

A part of you woke me
the other night
with thumbs poised
to gouge out my eyes –
call it nightmare if you will

What went before
is lost in subterfuge
and mental acrobatics

I have no time for fabrications
while honey dripped
from a mouth
more used to meat

and the ghost you loved
retreated in the house
already falling

♪

Betrayal

Break the silence of this night.
All learn that love is not –
only talk of it.

Your creation
your eyes observe the changes.

We seek you in flight
depth
action
thought.

And in your terrible serenity
you hear the stumbling on roots
stones.
Hear the echoes fading.

When sweat or blood
falls on the night –
town by town
village by village
pillow by pillow –
when cries are muffled loneliness
that piece of bread
dipped in bitter herbs
stands as a question mark
to the final glance of eternity.

House for Sale

The lady lay in decline
she never cared for embroidery
and the rook's raucous voice was not her choice
of music.
From the long windows of the drawing room
she counted the graves –
her husband used the inscriptions to teach
the children Latin.

When the cracks appeared
in ceilings and walls
she had become an inscription –
sons and daughters dispersed.

But their footsteps were left
pattering, thumping up from the brown painted kitchen
toward a corridor of dreams
that clung to every curtain.
And silence reigned – cruelly –
more alive than dead.

Song in January

this is the last time
it shall be said

crushed
with a battering ram
of words
a rack
of works
pulled apart
shoved into the ground

now on this plain of desolation
think back
relive
both sorrows
both joys

yet grievances
must be stripped bare
laid to rest

Bright the January sun
bright the January stars

At night
universe and sea meet
drawing us outwards

Without the breath of love
there is no life

Gardener's World

Behind clouds
other worlds walk
in spinning light

Midsummer begins slow
with birds' song
low mist over meadow

from the path by the greenhouse
scent of mist, tarragon and fennel

When you called me
I was only half awake

Demon Lover

For Dinah Livingstone

Once, I saw you
proud, mystical
wreathed in may and cow parsley
you were in contemplation
I dared not approach

and once you called my name
it echoed through the crumbling house
I crouched in the moss-covered courtyard –
hidden by tangled roses –
afraid to answer

So the moon grows above
the mountains in the clouds
no word has come
no sign

I stand at the secret gate
where the grass reaches my waist
I listen for steps of man or beast
hear only the wind sigh
in the evergreen trees

and then
nothing

♪

Christmas Horoscope

For Audrey Nicholson

Uranus rolls my past
into a ball and throws it
to Aquarius
Aquarius unravels the mess
and drapes what's left
around Taurus.
What would a bull
do with a red rag?
He makes two large holes
with his horns
and Jupiter magnificent in
gold lamé
chucks the rag out towards emptiness.

On the 22nd of December
Capricorn offers me
a pair of wings
'What to do with these?'
But the sun is in his eyes
and he doesn't answer.

All these different enlightenments
scattered above and below
confuse me.
The wings are an inspiration
but a little revolutionary.

'Truth,' says Virgo
'is something you must come
to terms with.
Don't worry about Uranus
he always was disagreeable.
What he considers true
is usually false.

Trouble is his second nature.
Give me the wings
and when you look at the January sky
you'll see
why you never spread them.'

The Last Tea Ceremony
of the Japanese Tea Master Rikyu

Clouds shift in dark sky
rain has fallen
the grass sparkles now
and faint perfume of
damp blossom mingled with incense
floats on the air

My feet on the wet path
soundless
heart beats a little quick

for one who believes in magic
this is a moment of moments
worlds stand still

And you beautifully greet me
palms together
you bow with a sad smile

I cannot match such dignity
hardly restrain my tears
'Heaven and earth are pitiless'

Perfect is the peace of your room
the red peony tended by delicate fingers
silently confirms
the kettle's song of praise

And the tea will not choke me
when you hand the porcelain bowl
I will drink like the others
without comment

But I can feel the breath of waning Autumn
when I receive your final gift
Beautifully you drain your cup
and mar tranquillity
by its shattered fragments

When the waves parted
a middle way was revealed
as we part
I can find no way

A cluster of summer trees
in pale moonlight
black iris stand sentinel
at your door

♪

Home Visit

For David Healey

It's the same for you, doctor,
she said,
all these pills and potions
spread out on the kitchen table
will do neither of us any good.

I am ready,
she said,
to turn my face to the wall,
or to the East,
or to the sun ...
deeply sad, doctor,
that's the root of it.

And yet ...
the strawberries,
she said,
warm, slightly gritty,
fingers smelling sweet of them.

The grey dawns with bird chorus,
clip clop of horse
when coming home on a summer night,
my heart –
or was it yours, doctor? –
turns over.

What you want
is the word made visible

or is that what I want?
Isn't that why you are here –
to tell me?

Searching for Noon's Repose
in Troubled Midnight

That you should stand there
unseen
shrouded in mist
endlessly beautiful.

The old stairs
with grass and wild flowers
growing in the cracks.
Bougainvillaea-scented air
and patterned sunlight
on the warm stone underfoot.

Surely it was not you
who turned away
but me –
not out of spite or malice
not because you remained so silent
hardly obtainable
almost a work of art –
Nothing of this ...

You understand there was no choice
I had to leave
had to turn away and face the shadow's sorrow.

Perhaps you wait
for my return
perhaps now you will walk out of the mist
place your flowers in my arms
and speak for the first time.

Snapshots from an Album 1884-1895

1

It rained that winter.
Later it snowed.
The Walworth Road seemed always slushy,
everything dark
as though the sun never shone.
No, the evenings were not inviting.

But for Great-Grandfather Charles,
with his brood of musical offspring,
the 'show must go on' –
and it did night after night,
the girls lifting their skirts
with one free hand,
lugging their violins, trumpets,
trombones or double bass
through mud and fog
to play Massenet, Gounod,
even Wagner at the Assembly Rooms.

A Strauss waltz brightened the drear hours
for the chestnut vendor
as he stood on a draughty corner.
He beat time with icy feet.

In the morning the butcher's boy
cycling through Camberwell
whistled *Alice Where Art Thou?*

2

Summer. South London left behind.
The family are now at Margate
or maybe Hastings,
relaxing for half an hour
outside the concert hall.

The girls are all smiles
the prettiest sports a parasol
and shows a glimpse of slender ankle.

Summer. Young men in boaters
stroll the promenade eyeing the ladies
whose white dresses flutter in the sea breezes
their hats trimmed with cornflowers.
Not a deckchair to be had.

And then the nightly concert
a popular event – all tickets sold.
The programme much the same
a selection of Scottish Airs, an extra waltz
and perhaps a Galop (spelt in French)
and Great Grandfather receiving
a standing ovation for his solo on the cornet.

3

Back in the Walworth Road
the family turn to spiritualism –
it must be serious
they've formed the Spirit Band
and Great Grandfather arranges concerts
every Sunday evening before the séance.
His youngest daughter sings

The Lost Chord
and his son plays *Life Let Us Cherish*
on the violin.

There is a picture
taken of the Medium,
a dearly beloved passed on
drifts behind his head.
She has a mass of white hair
but her legs are not visible
only the semblance of a white robe.

4

Great Grandfather Travelling through Brentford Meets with a Railway Accident

On December the 23rd
Great Grandfather is late arriving home.
His family sit up and wait anxiously.
The last train, the last tram
have come and gone.
Great Grandmother dabs her eyes
with a crumpled hankie.
Her sons pace the room.
On the table is a loaf of bread
a basin of dripping and a pot of tea
gone cold.

At last a policeman comes to reassure:
'Only slight injuries. Oh, yes
he'll be out of hospital in time
for Christmas lunch.'

'Get to bed, now, Mother,'
the daughters urge,
'we have a rehearsal early in the morning.'

5

Coming to Grief

Twice he noted this.
Once at Exmouth
and another time at Yarmouth.

Perhaps he faltered on the cadenza
in his famous composition
The Charing Cross Polka,
or maybe he had a sudden lapse of memory.
But here he's written:
'the fair one with golden curls' –
no knowing who she was.
All the photos are of family.

Not a guilty look from him
as he poses outside the kitchen door
in jaunty wide-brimmed hat
a Byron-type cravat around his neck,
cornet in hand and a faint twinkle in his eye.

6

Marriage is in the air.
Enter Nellie of 'the sweet voice'.
Not a great beauty but most suitable.
She's very gifted –

she plays the violin, trombone
and the piano.
Her plump musician's hands are capable.
She'll be a matriarch.

Great-Grandfather welcomes her
with a bear hug,
Great-Grandmother proffers
a soft cheek.
Brothers and sisters gather round
to offer seed cake and tea from
ornate china cups – the best.

Her future husband
touches his moustache, nervous
he will always be a little bashful.

7

An exciting moment
lunching with Elgar at the Grand Hotel.
He seems to approve of women musicians.
There they sit among the palms,
red plush and gilt chandeliers,
dressed to kill –
Nellie in black, the epitome of elegance.

Very different from the Camberwell Road
lunch a hurried affair in the kitchen –
leftover cold meat
hard cheese, a piece of bread.

Over-awed, sitting with Elgar
white napkins in pyramids
vases of flowers –

no one smiles.
Not even the waiter.

8

New faces appear.
Babies in layers of petticoat
gurgling under frilly bonnets
are held up to the camera
by adoring relatives.

Changes in family life –
one son married
another joined a symphony orchestra,
he visits home less often.

Great Grandfather's beloved twins –
red-haired beauties named after
musical instruments –
travel Europe with a Ladies' Band.

The next generation
their tiny ears filled with music
thump the kitchen table.
'Soon,' someone says,
'they'll be ready to learn the piano.'

First Steps

He had come
through Orion's belt
familiar with ducks
having seen them often
in the starry waters

Awake in his sarcophagus
he had observed the flight
of wild birds
and pondered on their journey

Now
memory plunged earthwards
with a wave of sunlight

told him
that walking was a way to life
and he smiled through swathes of cotton
surprised he could laugh
at being young again

♪

Psalm

How can I dare to want the feel of your hand
on my cheek
how dare to send messages with the swallows
as they dip furiously through pale evenings?

If the clouds are golden
it is because you have painted them

If my eyes are tired
it is because they search for you constantly.

That you live far beyond me
fills me with hope
and you must believe that I hope for little –

your voice, perhaps, murmuring in the night
your thoughts taking possession of mine
or that we might meet
on a train
or in a crowded restaurant
that we will meet on the border of sleep
and in the great emptiness
which comes at moments of supreme silence.

♪

Spell before Sleep

This is a great place for kindness
my love
despite the shouting and tyranny of the last word

Pay no attention to the broken walls
or the last scrap of potato skin
Only in dreams the food vanishes
and meals are late on the table

Only when darkness prevails
we dream that our beds are moved constantly
that dust covers us

Till morning my love
and when all is watery blue
we will find sun-apples

Our shuddering strength
spread out across daybreak

♪

Confession

It is my tongue
not my heart that fails to function
encased in a steel barrier

if only you knew
how thin the steel!

Fear is the root of evil
fear of misinterpretation
of drowning you in unwanted tears

So you move further away
while my tongue sticks bumbling –
and the crack in my heart widens

♪

Rain

Rain drips
from broken gutters
drips through the roof
through the ceiling
any crack it happens to find

On the lawn
a pheasant tries to hide

its head
its heavy feathers

The woman
moves from room to room
places a bucket
to catch the leaks
stares at the blotted sky

then
takes up her thoughts
where she had left them:

'It matters little
that so-called time
races onwards
or fills the day
with worries and
trivialities ...

the first apple tasted bitter
bitter and new ...
we were all new ...
Agape, love
those words came later
in God's old age'

♪

Leningrad

We sat in September sun
and watched an old woman
sweep the road with a broom.
Her black-scarfed head bent towards her work

she seemed not to notice us –
tourists gaping at St Isaac's.
Perhaps we saw her again, later
in the afternoon
her black-scarfed head
bent over one of the massed graves
as she placed her flowers
so tenderly on the smooth grass.

♪

Tübingen

A melancholy city
in spite of steep banks down to the river
and the sloping gardens
with vines, roses
and swans dipping their heads
past Hölderlin's tower.

We have often climbed
the cobbled streets
to the castle walls –
from here the concrete blocks of flats
sprawled across the landscape
are not visible.

The poet's gentle resignation
haunts us
scoffs at the opulence
and points to a man crumpled in the market place
crazed and ignored.

World Apart

The dream beneath the dream
was a river bank
the river deeper and darker
than the dream itself.

She dreamt of him
as he walked towards her
he paused, then smiled.

He dreamt of her
waiting
her hair blown by the wind
as in older dreams.

Summer dreamt of winter
shivering without leaves.
Winter dreamt of summer
heavy with sunlight.

The city enveloped night and day
danced between joy and sadness
roaring, shrieking against
the river's quiet brownness.

And the dream leapt beyond the city
lifted him, lifted her
out of time
out of world

that they should remember
their embrace
and her head on his shoulder.

Terra Firma

See how the sun glints on red juiciness
high above me!

My feet are on the grass
but my eyes look towards the top branches

If my ladder cannot be repaired
then the birds will share the cherries with angels

♪

Holding Breath

You breathe in
I breathe out
the oyster on the plate pulsates
until
you swallow it

You hold your breath
I hold mine
we are waiting for the pearl
to drop from your mouth

Relict

For Julie

Every morning when she woke –
sometimes joyfully –
she had expected ...
but what she expected she never put into words ...
more a feeling.

Every morning she cleaned her teeth,
washed her face,
because she had been told it was good to do so;
this applied also to the putting on of clothes.

Even now it was the same
and her expectancy continued,
though in an undertone.

From the window she watched
how the leaves flew from the trees.
It had been thus every year
endless years.
Her face, too, she realised
had an autumnal touch.

Driving home one rainy night
she had thought how it was when he
had sat beside her.
The thought came unawares
like the many thoughts she tried to block.

That he had been her life she would deny –
outwardly –

inwardly she bowed her head
acknowledging the truth

So on this night of rain
she spoke aloud her thoughts,
addressed his empty presence
with words which almost surprised her.

He had taken her life, she said,
drawn out her heart.
What was the use, she argued,
of an empty body or days overflowing
with nothingness ...

Since then the rain, the night,
woke with her every morning,
her day being over before it was begun.
Her tooth brush by the basin
clothes on the chair.

And through the window
she saw the trees
had no more leaves to shed.

♪

The Prisoner

He writes of falling blossom
lace on a woman's sleeve.
For hours, from his restricted view,
he observes the effect of snow or ice
on sparrows, pigeons.
He feeds a lone squirrel
with crumbs left from stale bread.

Delighted with the sun
he remembers walks he took in childhood,
fishing expeditions, picnics.

He studies the history
of each new place he's sent
his visits often short
but never sweet,
sometimes long and filled with bitterness.

Doctor Manette, locked in the Bastille
kept alive by making shoes.
After eighteen years he was recalled to life.

No comparison, you murmur,
the good doctor had done no wrong,
besides, times have changed.

How long, I ask,
can a punishment last?
Twenty-five years of slopping out,
twenty-five years of fear and turning keys.
Surely it's time enough for times to change?

Or should he die
yearning for hedgerows with primroses,
red tinged leaves of autumn
to fill the cracks in his cell walls?

Doctor Manette from Charles Dickens, *A Tale of Two Cities*.

Mothers, Daughters, Mothers

That she should sit by an open window
accusing herself of stupidity or worse
was a perpetual occurrence.

The wrong words formed on her tongue
always, or nearly so ...
what was spoken was spoken
dispersed, dispensed
leaving an agony of humiliation.

She was only too aware
that the eccentricities of youth
lose their charm with the years.

This longing to be loved –
loved above all else –
was a common experience –

the first human cry
and also the last one.

From many lives away
she saw the clouds suspended
over the pattern of changeable days

shadow and light
first and last
reflections of an eternal circle.

Doctor Meets Patient Again

'It seems,' he said,
'like yesterday,
at your bedside,
sleeves rolled up
while you moaned,
sweated, pretending
you enjoyed childbirth.'

Surprising
these threads of intimacy
still remain.

'And to remember
the colour of your hair
sticking to your cheek
and those long fingers
which dug into my hands.'

Ethically
the poetry in my mouth
silent.

February
the child's first cry
thirty-three years ago –
now June
and pink roses scratch
the window.

'Tell me then
where will you rest at noon?
For winter is past

flowers bloom again,'
he said,
quoting from the Hebrew.

♪

With No Man's Land Between Us

1089-1989

Sundown, soon to be night
homesick, battleworn
we have loaded our guns with Faith, Truth –

We fire across the fields and desert
and scatter to the four winds.

Guns, swords or words
'to purge the air
of the air we breathe'
or 'to rid the world of infidels':
it hardly makes a difference.

The act of death is ugly
and one fact certain
we are both human.

Do we kill what we fear
because of our ignorance?

A Cold Spell in October

In the night the wind flurried three strangers
as they prowled among old apple trees
the orchard gate creaked, disturbed a pheasant

Three strangers cloaked in night
stealthy on frosty grass

The farm doors are bolted
no lamp in the window

Three dead elms guard the sloping field
and round and about shadows waver

In the night a fox barked
in the frosty night a fox streaked over the fields
and the waiting vixen sniffed the air

♪

Ancestors

Not just the living roam here
the breathless ones gather
peer through the gloom
crowding each other

Curious and sympathetic onlookers
their prayers push away time barriers

On misty mornings
hear them whisper in the distant trees
and sigh on the stairs

Their touch is gentle
cold

They are never done with grieving

♪

Walking in Twilight

Yet I go on talking in
strange sentences
trying to entice you to a land
far off but nearer than you suppose.

Such mystifying words
only annoy you –
although the words include
the marsh and the dead bird
with elongated feet,
stiff and beautiful.

When night begins
each twig states an existence
alien to our own
purer, less muddied ...
clearly, seen on our walk home
late November evening.
The cold climbing from our feet
driving our very being
upwards and out
towards the first star.

One Another

For David Storey

The old man stands looking out
from the early hours
not sure what he wants
except to be wanted

Through the night
all the nights
his thoughts too quick
rushing, his mind dizzy

Only the amazing forget-me-nots
held peace
soothed turmoil
ever since
yes, that was it –
since he had understood
and laughed
very softly
not to alarm

What he understood
was a long way down
deep where forget-me-nots
touched his roots

and he could hear
standing looking out
could hear notes from the piano
something she had played
those years

when he had watched
through the window
Her form he remembered
with grace

Paused – then
'These are not my tears
I feel on my cheeks
as she stands
inside me looking out
waiting for the solitude to fade'

And through the night
his thoughts on an untidy lawn
so that when he closed
his eyes
the void was blue with stars

♪

A Slow Loving

My two-toed sweetheart
I have watched you through long nights
hanging amidst leaves
and at first mistook you for
a new, exotic flower.

The grace with which you move
so thrills me that my own grasp
on the bough where I cling in ecstasy
begins to falter.

I have watched you swim
through the swampy water

which matches your fur of various
shades – black, orange, green –
as it lifts and ripples in the ripples
you make with your steady strokes.

What fear have I of jaguars
if I can keep my eyes open
long enough to look at you?

Even eating seems a waste of effort
it distracts me from your presence.

Send me a sign, beloved,
I will come and share your life
if only for a while.
Send me a sign in time for me
to descend my tree and ascend yours.
Or, to give you time to descend yours
and ascend mine.
What you wish is my desire.

Oh, let us cleave together
as the creepers cleave and twine
above our heads.

Reading Lesson

For Eva and Paul Hoffmann

A is for aeroplane
B is for bomb
M is for man
Here is a baby

B is for baby and bomb.

Here is a woman
holding a baby
Here is a man
with a gun in his hand
H is for hand

W is for world
spinning in space
it is round like a ball
B is for ball
and for baby
also for border
This invisible line
is a border
and around it is country
Maybe it's your country
maybe you were born here
B is for born
also for baby, remember?
B is for border
and ball
C is for country
Are you comfortable?
C is for comfortable

What does it mean?
It means
B for bed
F for food
H for house
W for water
without these it is not comfortable
Are you comfortable?

If you cross the invisible line
B for border
you may find yourself
in someone else's country
C is for country
Perhaps the man with the gun
lives there
M for man
G for gun
He may not want you to stay
He may fire his gun
Perhaps he has no house
no bed
no food
no water
W for water
He is not comfortable
neither are you

Bullets fly
so do bombs
Remember B for both
They fly like birds

another B
and cross invisible borders
and large countries
very easily
where people
P for people
are not always comfortable

But this is history
beginning with H
like hand
We will close the book

and I will give you a biscuit
What letter does biscuit begin with?

♪

Suffolk Future

Once, those were trees
and this stinking tarmac
rolled long shadowed
in late sun
towards the sea.

Collar-doves
mournful all summer.

The worlds we inhabited
were separate
yet connected.

The house stood there –
just there
where cars and lorries thunder by –
the gate opened with a click
your skirt brushing against
willow herb
as you rang the bell.
You rang the bell, because
you said, it woke
the silence.

We walked along the cliffs
lit by brilliant gorse
and once, were lost for hours
in heather

looking for the path
to lead us home.

The sea splashes forlorn
on an empty beach
listening to the buzz of power.
This car park
is a garden of remembrance
where we sat on a worn bench
and counted butterflies
resting on the sunny wall.
The leaves, flowers, long grass
almost enveloped us.

Were we warned
did we warn anyone?
And the new world
miles and miles of concrete desolation
and talk of progress.

I search for you
my love,
in the deep of my head
not lost but gone before
as it were.

The Healing

Beyond the fields where a white horse plays alone
more fields rise and dip
as far as the eye can see.

Here, in the room, it is quiet, airless,

hands fill the spaces ...
my grandmother's hands were plump and kind
my mother's elegant,
father took pride in his filbert nails
his joints and knuckles large.

My own lie in my lap
bearing a family resemblance.

The hands on my back are also plump
oddly powerful
as the pain drawn to the surface
simmers upwards from my sweating neck.

The horse tosses his head
paws the ground, restless,
a car passes, seemingly on the horizon.

My family enter or rather
I enter them
connections now but no boundaries.

If it can be called 'appearances'
I see them from a distance in sepia.

My eyes are open
through a haze something parts company
with my body ...

the hands intervene
cover my eyes.

The horse stands motionless
under the quivering apple tree.

Orphic Nocturne

He walked, as often as not,
along the rough path
to the place that God made.

The afternoon was quietest,
heat drove other folk away.
Alone, he could contemplate
narcissus, orchid,
or wait for the green lizard
to venture from under the stones.

He was used at last
to his own company –
there was a time when silence oppressed him
when he had listened eagerly
for the sound of her step
or murmur of her voice.

Now the bird song
the rustling leaves
was all he needed in the way of company.

When he woke he could see
from his bed
the top of the mountain where rocks
had the shape of a fortress,
she had once told him tales
of an enchanted castle.

He remembered these stories
as he walked towards God's place
and the cuckoo echoed his laughter.

She, too, had walked this path
stopped sometimes to bathe her feet
in the stream
and pointed to the buzzard
as it dived down and down dizzily
between the mountains.

And colours –
she lived in a land of colours
she grew in fields of purple, pink, blue,
in air light as cleansing light.

And as often as not
he turned
quickly
half hoping to catch a glimpse of her.

Even as he paused
her strange presence disturbed him
as though she stood
as she always had
a little behind him.

The place that God made is a village, Dieulefit, in the southern part of
France.

Psyche

Even though she'd become 'a willing bride of death'
she hadn't jumped
no one had thrown her from the crags

She was wafted, so they say, by a 'gentle breeze'
Such a wonderful sensation, floating
through soft air
till she lay surprised in a scented peace

That was how she thought of it
that was how it began

Then the sound of wings
the loving darkness

She never actually confessed to loneliness

It was later
when she'd sorted red currants from white
and white currants from black
raspberries from loganberries –
careful painstaking
her fingers stained

Yes that was when
she became fully conscious of her plight
and wondered where Amor was
or if he'd ever been

And later still
when she wept over her cup of nectar

knowing she would remain
an unknown thread of silk
among the gods

♪

Sara Coleridge Speaks

The magnificent scenery,
which of course you describe magnificently,
has not gone unnoticed –
those starry nights
frost or snow glittering on the trees,
I, too, have remarked
as I walked back and forth
soothing a fractious baby.

Even on the rare nights
when sleep might be possible
your nightmare screams
would wake the dead.

You lie ensconced in your warm room
nursing your rheumatic legs
and other trauma,
between times write fascinating letters,
study philosophy and philosophise.
Dear friends come to visit you –
they rush to the kitchen
for enriching broth and look at me askance
because I am not fit to be your wife.

I loved you once,
but learned in those anguished months,
which you know nothing of,

that love, Samuel, is something
you don't understand for all your talk and verse.

And when your friends
brush past me in the kitchen
impatient, sneering,
I relive the time when, far off in Germany,
your work, your genius undisturbed
by messages of grief,
I rested my head
against the empty cradle.

♪

Omens

Yahweh's rage was immense
he tore the trees from his head
spat out the waves as they rose
in the mighty gusts of his sighs ...
his footstool trembled under his feet
his roar made Heaven shake.

This was not the first
nor the last time.

The prophet, on his knees,
bowed his head to the sand
and begged for mercy,
and Saul said:
'Yahweh's evil spirit
has swept across the reeds of my soul.'

That was not the last time either ...

Yahweh raved through the centuries
he sent his sons flying
in all directions
threatened often
to grind his image into dust ...

but Yahweh's head is balder
his breathing slower, heavier
his rage is calculating
For the first time
the prophets raise their heads
anxious
silent.

♪

An Antique Traveller Returns

Alone
listening
to the drip of moisture
in a tangled rain-forest,
the screech of monkeys
or flutter of fantastic wings

Alone
squelching through mud
leeches bothersome
and across lost deserts
my feet scorched

Sometimes
the sea just licks the stars
tenderly

singing them tales
of fabulous lands

Sometimes
golden leaves
fall from golden domes
miracles in sunlight

There are places
where old women kiss
the saints' bones yellowed
in a velvet coffin
My eyes have indeed
seen the glories of the Lord

Now here, under this mulberry tree
with time to reflect

I say that life
is a bridge
to be crossed not built upon
that love can be very terrible –
it can swallow you alive
torture you to death
but without it there is no
music
just a roll of drums

Psalm

Come
let me breathe your presence
since you have won me
discarded me
lifted me up
thrown me down

Because
the world is all darkness
cold and cruel
let me breathe you

But maybe
you are lost, alone
seeking a path
through fields of swords
and barbed wire

I keep sending
messages
trying to catch the grey winds

Communication
of the mind
is such a difficult thing

I thought you knew it

Monastic Interlude

The Cloister

Sleep invades the first hour
by seven the birds have ceased their chorusing
and sun begins to warm the frosted stone

Daffodils catch his eye
as he passes under the arch –
not by bread alone
not by any means

The sixth hour
and his prayer enters the primroses

Meditation

Memory fails from time to time
from year to year

But learning to forget
is a useful lesson
when trivia clog the soul

'The soul,' you ask, 'what's that?'

Nothing tangible exactly
can't be seen quite
yet I defy you to say it isn't there

Scriptorium

Thoughts arrive with the wind
fall from the sky
unhindered

nothing now
to write in the margin

a hand holds the pen
dictates what is written

sunlight in dusty stars
covers the manuscript

Herbalist

For every disease he has a remedy
the herbs plucked from his heart

Tulipa planted amidst lavender and thyme –
he says they are the veritable lilies of the field
which grew wild outside Jerusalem

Tulipa combat depression
Feast your eyes, he says
and your soul will be healed

Recreation

Here we sit
at liberty to talk
as we mend our socks

small talk
nothing personal

Finally dear friend
wouldn't you rather listen
to the music of the reeds?

Kitchen

The potatoes have been grown in silence
likewise the beans
In silence both are prepared
ready for cooking in heavy pans

A labour of love
served silently with bread and wine

The Great Fast

Not the bread
so much as the word
and not the word
so much as the tongue –
the tip ever ready for venom

but rise with the yeast
and the Word will hold you

Hermit

A remote cave
is no escape from world turmoil

which remains hidden in the inner man –
or inner woman
since Adam cannot be separated from Eve –

Solitary
he comes to terms with conflict
understands the meaning of Hell

Only then
a return to life becomes possible

Contemplation

Icons smile through incense
candles vie with the setting sun

The choir splits open the body
exposes bone
parts mind, heart and soul

Space is eternal

Mea Culpa

Beneath layers of lies
or pictures of justification
is a burnt wound
In light it heals
partially

Truth is no easy matter

Penance

Learn how to love
to give and receive

biting the dust leaves a bitter taste

The Porter

His hand
prevents the keys on his belt
from jangling

His felt-shod feet
noiseless
Who waits in the bitter wind
asking for shelter?

Across the marshland
the sea roars and pounds

Someone has knocked
trusting that the door
will be opened

Winter Saturday

Child of my child
holding my hand
we walked on the promenade
to watch the waves

There was no alteration
nothing happened
only our eyes met
in acknowledgment
as the blood ties
which unite us
quivered

♪

Talking to an Absent Friend in the Garden

Do you hear the dry seeds pop
small explosions in the air around us?
Do you hear the leaves whispering their love
to the elderly branches

I speak your name
expecting no response

Our worlds are far apart
yours may not exist
mine is a riddle which only you could solve

Curing a Hurt

Try sleep
Pillow down on a pile of leaves
seek oblivion for a while
On waking the hurt will be waiting
to hurt just the same

Time takes a long time to heal

♪

Solving a Problem

Seen in the light of chrysanthemums
it begins to look different
As they say 'things fall into place'
when planted firmly in the ground

Roses consider their growing
and lilies only fester in a vase

♪

Willow

From the Russian of Valentin Berestove

Willow
why do you curve obliquely
your green hair
almost touching the overflowing river?

I creep near the hollow bank
to avoid the axe
Beautiful willow
why would they cut you down?

The wood of my trunk
is needed for the bridge to be built
my space for the road –
so why bother with beauty –
where my heart is
there lies the treasure

Seven Deadly Sins

Pride

Not the odd glance in the mirror
nor a pat to a perfect leg
not the head held high
or knowledge of something well done
None of this is important
But beware of feeling indispensable
and that faint moment of superiority
Caught unawares the result is ominous

But it takes as long to reach Hell
as it does to reach Heaven

Gluttony

Just the thought maybe
makes the mouth water ...
a favourite chocolate
filled with marzipan – sweet almond heaven!
Or at night in agitation
you leave your bed
to eat that last piece of treacle tart
indescribably golden to the tongue
lonely on its plate in the larder

Lust

Sweat oozes behind the knees
it slithers down under the armpits
Heat, reflected from the glass roof
is damp, intense
and perfume of earth of plants
rises headily
Long fleshy leaves stretch out
from juicy stems
cherishing a flower
with curving petals, revealing
their furry texture
How the body throbs in sympathy
and abandonment at such a welcome

Envy

She spilt red wine
over my white dress
and her boyfriend spoke sharply
her smiling apology
spread with the stain

Avarice

I want to keep you all to myself
everything you possess
must belong to me
down to your last finger-nail

Anger

He took a whip
and chased them from the temple

Is it possible
to be righteous
and sinful?

Sloth

While the child floated
downstream
they relaxed in the warm garden
chattering of this and that
half awake to the ripple of water

Letter from the Dead

How sad
to wander around the house
not noticed by you

How cold
and silent your presence
Your tears fall inwards
I cannot wipe them away

Side by side
we look out of the window
I watch the grass quivering with life
the buds already forming on the trees
I feel the slow rhythm of the earth
the strong and weak heart-beats
all around us

There are many things to be said
but your ears are not
tuned to my voice

The prayers you send out –
little puffs of smoke vanishing into December –
swirl above my head

These words
I breathe onto the cobwebs
hoping they will be deciphered

Your future my dearest friend
is as uncertain as mine
No comfort there

But I will stay near you
kiss your cheek
knowing that when I do
you will shudder and say:
Someone just walked over my grave

♪

The Surprise

And God said:
Let them be pushed
through a corridor
into the light
ready
to be pushed
through a corridor
into the dark

My image
shall haunt them
all their brief days
I have created
therefore
I will destroy

Hope shall be their despair

Fragments from a Torn Tapestry

Based on the Paston Letters

Complaint and Request – A Young Wife

Send me a kirtle
sweet lord,
and a fair ribbon.
Let the kirtle be blue
of a goodly wool –
there's a chill in the house
as the days draw in.
The plums are preserved
the apples stored.
Quiet days pass
in a golden haze.
Hasten home I beseech
our bed feels sad
and I miss your smile across the table.

Sweet lord
why do you tarry?
Autumn is passed
heavy frost lies on the trees
it freezes my heart.
My cousin Agnes
holds her first born
in her arms
whilst I, forlorn wife,
watch green woodpeckers
swoop over the lawn
and feel the throb
of an unfilled breast.

Serenade
Night
descends deeper into time
the moon drops from the sky
raindrops change key
become tender
ever varying.

Take my hand
dear heart so full of love,
will you not journey with me
to the sun
where music is a blaze
of trumpets?

The Prison

Give me
the moment that never happened
the day that never came
the past that never was.

That way there is no reliving
no wastage
and then
even the most miserable dog can wag its tail.

Winter Farm

Mud frozen hard
stars still shining
the church clock strikes five.
Ah! the wind attacks the very soul

dizzy with it he staggers to the byre.

His wife stirs as the sky lightens
sighing in the knowledge of a cold hearth.
She scrapes frost from the window
watches the hens slither across ice.

Love and marriage separate
with advancing years.

Pilgrimage

We have been to Walsingham
the last mile on our knees.
We have purchased a fragment
of Our Lady's robe
and have been granted
a thousand years off Purgatory
in the priest's own hand.

Now we pray
that God can read.

Holiness

And the priest
is a merry fellow
full fat and gentle
he preaches not of Hell
but bids us love all men.

But why
when he lies under the mutilated willow

by the hedge
is he leering?

London

In the great city
is much noise and stench.
Of business here
I can say little
for in these hard days
no man is to be trusted.

Our masters tell us:
'Make yourselves friends of Mammon'
therefore many are betrayed.
Alas! it is true that
Judas does not sleep.

The Storm Blythburgh

Sky darkening
and then the wind
from far off
far over the sea sweeping waves, sand and pebbles
against the cliffs
on leathern wings

And we heard it coming
had no fear
being in God's house
Louder it came
shrieking among us
licking us with fire

swift and terrible
as the great beams tumbled
Two men died that day

Later
we found a huge handprint
blackened on the North door

On the Roads

If you would visit us
come not alone
but bring trusty servants
to protect you from danger
These are the King's highways and byways
these are the horses
these are the carts
these are the feet
some well shod
some beggared
that journey on business
pleasure of pain

If you would travel
from London to Norwich
it will take you three days
sweet cousin of mine

The Loving Cup

Good wife Joan
in a red petticoat
passes the jug of beer
with a sly smile
My Lady Margery
almost swoons with joy
under the flowering cherry
as her knight enters the orchard

John Jeffery lies shameless
behind the barn
with an over-loved whore
and our Lord Chamberlain
Ah! God forbid!
cries out against fornication
as he accidentally fondles
a maiden's breast

He is right we must at all costs
preserve a family life
But we all go lusting
in the spring time

In the Churchyard

Nothing to hide
only the wish for a mantle
to wrap the soul
Twelve hours
midnight to midday

let it pass
I counted seven lapwings in the field

Heavenly voices
across the reeds
and when they sing
the birds are silent

February for the Crazy Pilgrim

We danced and sang
our voices soared into the night
Eight danced
twelve danced
all numbers being sacred
We kept tune with grace
celebrating life's perfection

And then I thought
how fear is a great enemy
and I cried: Get thee behind me!
I'll not creep through each day
head bowed, feet tentative
Away with the amulets
sprigs of mistletoe
white heather
there's no place for superstition

In the sky the uncountable stars
lit up the melancholy of our fate
No wonder that we sang until
the whistling sands were stilled

Praise be to the morning sun
falling on the aconites

The Crazy Pilgrim in Conversation

Excuse me, comrade, I have lived for a specific period
and would be merry more often
if I could be acquainted
with this journey which began on foot

It is remarkable
to conceive a desire for a new life
when the present one is only slightly worn
but I am fearful of losing myself
losing the world would be no loss
but imagine losing oneself
imagine looking in the mirror
and not being there

Let me whisper in your ear
take stock of our surroundings
have you ever thought
that we might be in Hell already?
That the talk of paradise, utopia
is a leftover dream
from when we were flesh and blood?

No? Well living one's life, comrade,
is not as easy as crossing a field

Now I must continue the trek
thanks for your company
and remember the moment our shadows
touch the moon
we'll be laughing

On the Train

No longer at ease
in a city
my eyes and ears
are alert for danger
which leaves the burden
on your shoulders

Now in the solitude
of approaching winter
I think how we die bit by bit
at all our partings
how every numbered hair
on our heads
is recounted lovingly
with its change of colour
how the sparrows fall
are lost but cherished

Ah! the forbidden names
of God
how careful we are
to avoid them

Message from a Far Country

Mainly the news from here
is of hedges hacked to death
the first cuckoo of spring
and a green woodpecker sighted near the house

An escape from the horrors
which are reported daily in the media
no worse than what has gone before
but no improvement

So now I remark only on the rain
or lack of it ...

We seem to drift apart on some vast ocean
dreaming of a safe haven

When we finally land
I think we will not recognise each other

Cold Summer

Demeter is back in her cave
sulking. She is afraid that her daughter
has eaten yet another pomegranate seed.

For the last two years
Hades has dominated,
ignoring the agreement.
Persephone looks much paler
and the joyful spring in her step has gone.
At the moment she is resting.

Demeter looks out at the grey skies
and watches the corn lashed by winds.
Rain has made everything greener
and it has been a good year for poppies,
but, she thinks bitterly,
that's one of her son-in-law's favourite flowers.

What's Zeus up to? she wonders.
He's been making the earth quake
and sending fiery darts into forests.
Is it time for the end of the fifth race,
his Iron Men? Will he crush them
and burn them from the face of the earth?

My earth, she cries, where my hands tend
orchids, wheat and wild berries,
earth my brother gave me along with our child.
Our child light, fragile as apple blossom
crowned and married to death.
A promise of hope as a wedding gift.

Undressing in front of Chekhov

For Vernon Rose, who gave me the first line

This is the house that Chekhov wrote
and in the lamplight
a woman stands in her petticoat
contemplating the man she loves.

Far away from Yalta
or Moscow,
in this dacha built on marshy ground,
where laughter and tears
follow a human pattern
and the souls of beautiful women
gaze from windows waiting for something
which might happen,
he watches the nightly ritual
amused as clothes fall to the floor.

Is he aware of the axe
taken to rain-forests,
cherry trees almost forgotten
water and air no joking matter?

An observer now across a century
his voice out of silence:
'It seems to me that when I die
I shall still have a share in life.'

The Uninvited

These wild horses
which stampede from time to time
through my house and garden
demand to be fed,
vie with the peacock,
the guinea fowl,
claim attention.

To enclose them
in promises of heather-covered moors
proves useless,
to plead work or declining years
only laughable.

They trample on skeletons
not understanding bones,
they know nothing of reality,
nothing of evil.

Uncanny, sensual
they toss their manes,
enticing what is born of the spirit
to rise up and worship an alien god.

Demon Lover

No face
only a presence.
Darkness covers him
yet his invisible strength
holds no kindness.
I never know when next he'll pinion me.
He lurks by my shadow
laughs at my protest
with a hand stifles my screams.

His love pursues me through the years
posing as a tree covered in blossom
a flower with a trembling heart
or a robin with an eye full of questions.

Then he is upon me
breathing deeply into my ear.

Only last night he sneaked into the bed
grasped me tight
conjuring a village and villagers
who could neither see nor hear me.

Coming to Terms with Demons

Mostly they come by night
when the mind is busy.
They land on the bed
with a thud that could wake the dead.

Naked and furry
claw hands and human face
their weight almost stops all breath
a grimace covers the eyes.

On waking limbs are rigid
life slow to return.

These manifestations are a reminder
that three blind maidens spin their web of fate
beneath the roots of the world.

Switch on the light
with dawn the gargoyle leaves.
Now you can breathe again
your past drowned in waters of forgetfulness
your present here
your future lies in other hands.
There must be no despair.

♪

Tit for Tat

He told me:
'You could knock me down with a feather.'
So I did.

Not a large feather
not an ostrich or a peacock
more the size of an owl's.

What people say
or what they mean
is often questionable.
Taking him at his word
came as a shock to him
so when I turned my cheek
he hit the other one.

♪

Brief Encounter

Anima and Animus
met in the bathroom.
He took no interest in her naked body.
Unconcerned
she washed under her arms
and noted how he cleaned his teeth.
His face was blurred
hers, he hardly glimpsed.
'This makes more sense,'
he said,
'than carrying plates to Lowestoft.'
She asked him if he remembered
living in Balham.
No reply.
The building was too public
too many corridors,
Anima preferred a more intimate setting.
Her romanticism always annoyed him.
Animus made off into the night

knowing
she would wait
ever patient
for his return.

♪

Parting

Morning reveals a dead fly
stuck to the window
and wasps snuggling between curtains
whilst a butterfly flusters
around the stove

We've said goodbye often enough
too often
returned again
smiling
with tales of adventure

And now sun
warms the naked trees
lights up a magpie's wing
lessens the icy touch of wind

Perhaps any disagreements
evaporate with early frost
no one can say
if our last goodbye
was final

A Quarrel

A shadow comes between us,
our wills have clashed
leaving me quite incredulous.
Your quiet anger has completely dashed
my hope of lasting friendship.
Foolishly, I thought our minds
were linked in fellowship
not to be torn by winds
of words – right or wrong.
But now you have an axe to grind
leaving me no heart to search among
your past letters which were kind
full of your gentle humorous
soul, which now seems venomous.

♪

A Dream of Pride

What's to be done
with a king who smells of blood
is said to be holy
yet wants to conquer the world?

Marooned in a castle perched on a mountain
below him a plain criss-crossed with streams
his infantry, cavalry, tanks
his pikes, arrows, guns
whatever weapon in season

From his dreaming spires
snug, smug, this king offers gifts

to the oracle and unimpressed by enigmas
orders more soldiers into the fray.

But always when thunder darkens the sky
crashes into his sleep
the gods reveal themselves
to prove that no man while he lives can be happy
no man mightier than they.

And his son or his daughter
left behind, bereft of speech
holds a bunch of withered flowers
to place on charred bones.

The Haunting

What were you doing, Savonarola,
on that dark staircase,
doors closed on every landing?
The look you gave me as you sidled past
would have sent me to the stake.

So many people on the stairs
so many monks and priests
and continuous tramp of feet.

The house, tall and foreign,
a cobbled courtyard, long windows.
Not a monastery more a cheap hotel.
One or two old ladies,
garbed in black, gossiping with chamber-maids.

You were there mingling in crowds

of new arrivals
your cadaverous face easily recognised
under your cowl.

What were you doing, Savonarola,
in my dream, bidding me welcome
your voice sepulchral?

No flaming sword
no mention of plague or destruction
only people scurrying hither and thither
through murky technicolour.

And you continued down the stairs
leaving me to the final scene of nightmare.
A rope already round my neck
and a child pleading for my life.

♪

George Eliot's Piano Tuner

Tall, thin and consumptive
a lost genius?
Or plump, balding, with podgy hands,
very respectable,
with a son learning the trade
and a daughter learning the piano?
We have no photograph,
no name,
no family background
and but for the annoyance caused
no other mention.
How inconvenient
for the piano tuner.

He must have been quite ill,
very ill,
to have ruined the elegant wallpaper
and the carpet.
Perhaps he ate too many vol-au-vents
at his previous client's
on an empty stomach.
Or maybe the colours in the drawing room
chosen with painstaking care
offended him.
Or was he drunk?
His ears as dizzy as his head,
and disliking the duet played
by the ladies of the house.
We shall never know the true story.
He was discovered
sent home
(if in a cab who paid?) –
much in disgrace,
probably dying of T.B.
or mortification,
his reputation lost –
while the famous fussed and fumed
and asked Mrs Beeton
for hints on removing vomit
from silk wallpaper.
One might be permitted
to call the whole episode
a complete wash-out.

In 1863 George Eliot and G.H. Lewis moved into a new house in St John's Wood. Lewis, in a letter to a friend, wrote: ' ... besides the trouble and vexation incident to moving we have had extra annoyances. The piano tuner was sick over our elegant wallpaper, which Owen Jones had decorated, and over the carpet.'

Elgar

For Esme Sillito

Unless it was his mother's heart-beat
words were his first music.
Then as the sun burnt through the mists of summer
birds taught him harmony.

The wand of youth
conjured magic from early grass in spring,
first snow floating to transform
a dark world to one of dazzling light.
Woods around the house filled with melody.
Even the suburbs became a dream
pavements shining blackly in the rain,
and smells of fruit, vegetables
and new-baked bread drifting
from the market place of childhood.
All this apart from musical evenings
surrounded by a loving family,
their speech unhurried, life taken
at a *tempo più lento.*

He belonged to another land
and to those who do remember
it has become nostalgic,
seen through a haze of roses.

The dreams of genius came true
but without Alice he would not have risen
above the Malvern Hills.
Son of a piano tuner, married above him –
she fed him on tender care,

quiet in the home – all things flourished
and he drank with a glad heart
until his voice broke from its earthbound roots.

And still his soul was sad.
When the violin or cello cried out for it
his audience sighed, impatient
waiting for more pomp and circumstance.
When he obliged they made him Knight,
Baron, Master of the King's Music
and his soul grew sadder.

After she died
he walked in late autumn
under the trees in brown afternoons
thought of the soft skin on her neck
where her necklace lay.
Those words never spoken.

A last adagio orchestrated in his brain
not meant for human ears,
celebrated by trees
the copper of beech
knotty trunks of oak
vibrating in wild winds
blown from nowhere.

Night Life

In the hotel
guests wander aimlessly
enter rooms without knocking
some faces are familiar
but remain nameless –
not one of them casts a shadow

When morning comes no sun rises
the electricity fails

The word 'escape' on many lips
but how do you escape
from open doors, polite bell-boys
friendly chamber-maids?
All paid for by an unknown donor?

Ash-trays need emptying
everywhere chaos
little to recommend this place
a labyrinth of corridors

An old French lady tells me
she has enjoyed her visit
she offers me a box of half-eaten chocolates
then she adjusts her hat
and seems to evaporate
between two beds and a table

Tea Dance

There is a nostalgia in my soul
for a world without atomic bombs
for things which are small, polite
and harmless.
Please take my arm
together we will fight
the growing tedium of responsibilities
the creeping danger to the bones and face –
an afternoon's escape from those we love
to dance and dance again
touching
light as you will
with eyes averted.

♪

Nellie, my Grandmother

Nellie would have scorned Women's Lib.
She had been liberated for years,
had earned her living from an early age.
No prude, she was down to earth,
gave sound advice.
'Never let your husband know that
you can even boil an egg.'
And: 'Heaven help the woman who marries a virgin.'

Secretly she may have despised men
her father a wastrel and bully,
her husband weak.
When great-grandfather died
she took the family in hand.

Her house in Rowfant Road became its centre.
Packed to overflowing with sisters, brothers,
aunts, uncles and cousins
music seeped through the walls
out into the street.

Children played among grimy flowers,
children practised on an upright piano.
Nellie played her trombone in the bedroom,
Ernest his violin in the kitchen.
Ernest went down in the musical world
while cousins went up, one with her flute
to impress Ethel Smythe,
one, later, with his trumpet
to a prestigious orchestra.

Those in between worked where required,
overtures and interval music in theatres –
ah, those were the days! –
Lyons Corner House or Zeeta's tea rooms.
And some in a band on Clapham Common.
It was pleasant to take tea or lunch
whilst a trio played snippets from Schubert.
Or to stroll across the common
on a fine Sunday evening
and hear a selection from *La Traviata,*
scent from the Rose Garden wafted in the air.

What do you do all Day
while I'm at School?

For Leah, my granddaughter

Did you expect me to list
the potatoes in need of peeling,
what fish I choose for lunch
or how many times I dust the rooms?

No, no, awake or asleep
I dream, my love,
as most of us do.
Dream of golden horses in fields of cowslips,
peace in a land always beautiful
no wars, violence or hurt.

Like you, I withdraw from the world of reality
my hands grope for the path at night
my feet tread carefully to avoid lines.
Spaces fill with crotchets, quavers
a melody to rise
over dizzy mountain slopes
where prayer-wheels whirl and clatter
and rhododendrons riot.

Cathedral Revisited

For Richard

We have come to bury our dreams
in this cathedral of solemn music
our open coffin, carried by toy horses
halts before the priests robed in gold and crimson.
Clowns tumble down the aisle
their cartwheels faster than life itself
and cover our dreaming bodies with a mass of flowers.
Perfume fills our lungs
daylight bursts through the roof.

We walk out towards another church
built of different brick
where more priests wait –
oh, how patiently they stand
gazing into debris from a thousand bombs.

I wrap you with my last strength
and the last remnant of my pride
to protect you from evil.
We walk through autumn
already a breath of winter
Wisdom is beyond me.
We must find the magic place
where clouds can be brushed away
with sleight of hand.

Instead of Writing to You

For Hans Raimund

The wind is mournful
tired of worrying the sea into a frenzy
Instead of writing to you
I am thinking of the fishermen
who told me they get cold six miles off shore
they couldn't swim
The one who spoke had brown eyes
not blue
I tried to find the sea in him
He sold me sprats
dead cod in fish baskets
shivered my heart

You made me aware
of the maypole ribbons
danced by the wind
December sun casting blueness
on puddles deep in the farmyard

And the music of your marriage
played in our house
one summer
sings out from the frozen roses

For Dinah who is Glad
God is not in her Garden

The sun broke through the clouds
and now late afternoon warmth enfolds this garden.
A symphony of bees, flies, birds
join the rustle of leaves
and I think of you lying in the orchard, drowsing.

Fantasy on my part
because you are in London
possibly having tea in your own garden
glad of a respite from work
and sheltered from noisy traffic.
'No heavenly callers please'
written firmly on your gate.

And yet –
we search for the same thing
utopia, God
what's in a name?
We praise buttercups, foxgloves
recognise the Word
our prayers, too, mingle between fields of poppies
and buddleia growing from cracked walls.

Dichotomy

For Eva Hoffmann

Perhaps it is the darkness
the division of the soul
or the confusion of aloneness
in a place teeming with life

Some say it is weakness
to see two sides of everything
but still I take the middle way

In your face – tranquillity
in your presence
ordinary day-to-day activities
become illuminated

Shopping with you in a supermarket
supper on the balcony, candles lit
to keep away mosquitoes,
moments which have become important in my mind
struggling to reach an understanding

To be a participant
in a world of human horror
and a perfection beyond words
is almost a miracle

In Memoriam

Father Lucian Gafton 1996

The sparrow has found its nest
the swallow flown from the vale of tears

rises
leading the way to a misty world
where silence stands on the point of a needle

Leave behind your memories
joy or sorrow
few of us are saints

Ask nothing
replies come without questions
in a smile or a wisp of smoke from a cigarette

I will see your shadow on the summer grass
hear your voice as a cloud passes
and my body too
will tremble under the sycamore tree
and its heart lie quiet
in the faintest of sighs

♪

Death on the NHS

Tests were carried out
pills prescribed
old people patched up
along with their old cars.

What amounts to an overdose is an overdose
even when unintentional
what amounts to carelessness
is a lack of caring
which leads to feet turning blue under the blankets.

The end was a shattered lamp
paramedics trampling broken glass
and kindness underfoot.

You can't see the dead without an appointment
and with one you must wait
but not here
half in, half out of a busy ward
with telephones ringing
nurses scurrying and raised voices.

Grieving relatives are in the way
especially those who ask questions
especially when doctors
are wanting a post mortem.

We had a last glimpse of her
laid out by a red curtain
hands folded, respectable
not so very peaceful.

Here's a paper hankie
you can't have a glass of water
the carafe is empty.

Past Love

1

Sometimes I still think of you.
It began one afternoon
after your concert.
Vienna wasn't it?
Vienna in the snow.

In a cafe where I sat with friends
eating Sachertorte
you came and handed me a bunch of roses
clicked your heels
spoke tenderly in German
knowing I wouldn't understand.

Our friends teased you
laughed at my blushes
and outside, the snow
thickening on grey pavements
commenced the caprice in a minor key.

2

There is a less romantic scene.
Waiting for you to arrive,
your first visit to my home,
I saw from the window
my great aunt teetering down the street
her black hat awry
her black skirt trailing in the dirt.
And cruelly, in tears,

I begged my mother to intercept her
take her off, somewhere, anywhere but here
where my lover might be shocked
by a drunk old woman
on an unexpected day-return to London
lonely for her relatives.

3

You took me to the opera one July
and afterwards we walked across Hyde Park –
summer night in London, warm and smelly.
Under a lime tree you stooped to kiss me.
Suddenly police whistles blew.
'They're clearing the park,' you said.
We ran and as we did courting couples
appeared as if from nowhere
all of us running madly
stumbling from bushes, under trees.
At the gates by Rotten Row,
breathless with laughter,
we wondered why for those five minutes
we'd felt like criminals.

4

Rather than words
a hazy picture hangs on the wall
of my mind – the Green Room
at Wigmore Hall – I came
with the crowd of well-wishers
to murmur or rave about your fine performance.
You were surrounded by people I did not know
culture vultures, critics.

Elated, you flashed your smile
at all and sundry.
Our love, I thought, will be over
as quickly as a scherzo played at speed.

5

In bed you were delicate
your phrasing as perfect as your timing.
Melody flowed through your finger-tips
to bruise my heart for ever.
You never raped me
(another man did that at a later date).

6

Days would pass
without my hearing from you.
Angered and sad
I excused you, ready to pretend I understood
but once I saw you in a busy street
with someone else. Dark and chic
she gazed at you with adoring eyes
and you were too absorbed
to notice me slip by.

7

In the end I freed myself
cut the threads
refused to see you.
Oddly enough it was you who wept,
a spoiled boy

wanting something you couldn't have.
And so we parted.
Undramatic, unmusical,
no swan song
only a brief phone call
and then – silence.
But still I think of you
from time to time
in London
or Vienna
your long hands on the violin.

Encounter with Hermes

Long ago
alone in the mountain by Delphi
on his winged feet he flew to me
I leant back into the scent
of wild garlic and narcissus.
His voice
deep, loving, caressed my ear
fluttered my hair.

High in the blue
an eagle perched on a craggy ledge
his eyes bright.

Who would believe
how the earth revolved
in my hot blood
and arms of liquid gold
embraced my nakedness?

Who would believe
in a dream sent from Olympus
to a tourist misplaced by fate?

We bathed in a stream
its banks overgrown with flowers
unfamiliar blue and white.

He flew away to the world
of Shining Ones
paused by the temple of Apollo
to listen to music played
on strings of sun.

And I took a path
back to the valley
a winding path of stone and moss
stopping to pick up fragments
of broken idols
as the air cooled and Artemis
lifted her bow.

Aphrodite

With a look
I can transform
a sensible mortal
to a gibbering idiot

At my altar
heroes fall
swooning
in the fragrance of my incense

Alexandros
poor wretch
worshipped a woman
whose face resembled mine

Beware
of my beautiful gentleness
it can be deadly
with Eros' help
I shatter more than Troy

The Serpent to Eve

My scales are fantastical
so glad you admire them
and how clever of you not to touch me
with hot, sticky hands.

I confess you are as handsome as I am,
from the first moment of your creation
I loved your smooth skin,
and I have loved your curiosity
your self-reliance.

That companion of yours
he is a different matter.
No proper energy, so dull,
he hasn't dared examine this tree
where I coil myself to catch the sun.

Let me tell you a secret.
It's not the fruit
but what the fruit provides
is why you're forbidden to eat it!
Ah, your eyes widen!

Imagine, dear Eve,
what power is like
imagine having powers to match
you know Who!

Naomi to Ruth

We look into each other's eyes
I see your soul
you, mine.
Our own are as alien as the fields
where we have wept
with the loneliness which love
inevitably brings
and with the homesickness of old age.

We are bonded
by the same image
divided into flesh and bone
reflected in the many mirrors on your skirt.

Perhaps words should be
as colours on a canvas
joys and sorrows depicted there
for sharing.

Wife, daughter, mother, sister,
our names
threaded from light year to light year –
we are wiser than the next generation.

The Hard Core

Why send me here?
This is the convent of the Golden Heart
where it's obligatory to possess a heart of gold.
My feet stick in the generosity and kindness
which flows from the inmates onto the floorboards.
The sweet forgiving voices sicken me
they speak of casting out devils
and healing the sick.
And their prayers, ah God! their prayers
imprison me in ropes of silk.
I scrub and cook in penance for my many sins
guilty of not choosing the better part.
I am eaten alive by sanctity.

But in a moment of recollection
it occurs to me that gold is hard
can lead to misery and crime
is used for crowning teeth which bite.

If my heart was ever gold
it must have melted in the furnace
they call Hell.

Jairus's Daughter

People ask:
What was it like?
Was it light
or dark
did you hear voices?

Father says:
Go on, tell them.
His side locks have turned white.

And I thought of the sun
hot as Hell
on the beach where the boat landed
and the wailing women
were vultures smelling carrion.

Later I met Lazarus
our pain mingled
in an olive grove
we had no need to speak.

Birth and death
hold no meaning
for those who chase after the wind.

The Other Lazarus

There is a great gulf between us
from the moment of our birth ...
my sin was poverty
yours thoughtlessness.
Wrapped in a sleeping bag
I lay on your doorstep, burning with fever,
too ill to drag myself away,
too ill even for speech.
I couldn't beg and no one asked me
if I would like some water.
Sometimes a stray dog ambled up
whined in sympathy and licked my face.

In the arms of Abraham
I see your soul far off
burning in the agony of remorse ...
Lucky, unlucky, life was a game of chance
with obstacles bound to come ...
and now my peace is shattered
by your voice crying my name.

Crossing Over

It is not forbidden
to go from dark to light
or light to dark
but not encouraged
until the right time

Those who do visit
say little of what they saw
some mention the light
or the dark
some mention a welcome
some murmur of stepping into a smile

On return
the sun shines differently
a quietness falls
even fear evaporates
when the sea rages

No maps are needed
no trekking over mountains
or efforts to scale Mont Blanc
bridges are fictional
so are rivers

Strange how everything melts away
on the border

Washed Up

Sun shines on the sand
the sea blue-grey
and trees rejoice
birds hardly cease their love song

But caught in shallow water
he flounders
panting with an effort to survive

How had it come to this
how could he have imagined
when manoeuvring seas
heavy or placid –
his natural habitat –
that he would land up here

Somewhere in the deep
companions send messages of music
profound music
which Seraphim and Cherubim
understand so well

On the edge of immensity
he begins to fathom
the rhythm of waves
and voices of planets

Too late for regrets
or change
all this time he has dreamt of living
and all this time
he has been busy dying

His body becomes unfamiliar
dry, colder, he can feel it wither
his eyes
dimmed
survey a lost world
and he swallows its beauty
as he would a shoal of fish

♪

Credo

For Paul Hoffmann

As the morning star began to fade
a woman raised her arms
to proclaim the wonder of creation

All things in the heavens
under the sea
and on earth
are confounding, I agree, Lord,
down to the finest detail
no wastage
and to dust we shall certainly return.
Your plan for us is an enigma
we are left with doubts

I have not denied your existence
only marvelled at the evil and the good
which you control
marvel that you took part in the suffering
imposed on us
Strange and dreadful are the powers of Mammon
is that your other face?

Nothing contains nothing but you contain all.
The seagulls laugh when I ask for understanding
the starlings chatter among themselves
amazed at my ignorance

Into the darkness shed some light
for the path you indicate
is hardly wide enough for a soul to pass

In your extraordinary nothingness
take my love with its many facets
imperfect and at times ridiculous –
the tenuous link which holds me to you –
let it grow with the bursting of spring
with the heart of summer
the grief of autumn
the final ice of winter
then say again:
She has loved much

Finale

These hills are no place for cowards.
Look down – there lies the river
we must cross, no bridge provided
impossible to swim.
Strangely dark and menacing the water
as it gushes over slimy boulders
which are the stepping stones.
The trials so far endured
you've half forgotten.
But now do you notice how ominous the silence?
The emptiness? Not a bird, nor butterfly. Not one.
What lies ahead is Trial by Desolation.
How you cringe! Take cheer,
my timid soul, we've come this far,
no turning back, as you well know.
Pause here for a moment where sunlight
warms our backs and remember
how we floated across meadows
overgrown with daffodils, cowslips
all your favourite flowers
jumbled together out of season.
Remember how flying suddenly became easy
and there we were above ourselves, weightless,
light as dandelion seeds blown on a summer's day.
It grows dark.
No audience left, the curtain falls
before we're done.
We must descend, we've rested long enough.
Gather your courage
soon you'll be alone, without my company
but till we part you'll cling
to my last scrap of flesh.

Hearing Things

For Michael

Look,
there's a prose poem growing in that tree
mingling with the roses which have climbed
almost to the top.
Yellow roses, old-fashioned
and sweet-scented.
Can you hear the poem?
If you listen carefully it speaks for itself.
No, I never planted it,
it seeded itself along with the campion
and the hollyhocks.
This is a wild garden where plants happen,
are content to be left alone.
Unusual to have poems in trees?
Not really. The birds read them
before they settle for the night.
They sing them aloud, learn them by heart.
At first light every word becomes clear.

Help!

When he pierced her with a look
she dropped her eyes on the ground
and was lost.
He had turned head over heels with love.
A pity she couldn't see him,
his acrobatics were amazing for a man of his age.

She tried to speak
but was hindered by her heart
which was in her mouth –
it felt large and tasted horrible.

Glued to the floor, embarrassed,
he was unable to move
except his head which was still spinning.

Naturally he didn't lift a finger to help her.

Airborne

The pilot tells us
we are ready for take-off.
Farewell to the mountains,
the lake with its many borders
and friends who kissed us yesterday.

Memory loses its way
in the crowded streets
of towns visited too often.
Now it fades in swirls of cloud.
All journeys are double-edged –
all landings, whether smooth or bumpy,
hold an element of fear.

God knows where we'll fly to next,
we hope somewhere calm and pleasant
where sheep may safely graze
and trees recite poetry.

Castles in the Air

The traveller
from far off
has seen the pinnacles and towers.
The road he's followed
has been long.

The castle could be a mirage
of his tired brain.
What he hopes for,
whether it be pleasure
or pain,
remains his secret.
He still has far to go.

Now he is fading
into the mist
which hovers uncertain
at the end of day.

Quick, if you want to question him
run, grab his coat.
Ah! too late. He's gone.
These dreams,
how they cling
and how beautiful the moon
hanging in the air.

Settling Matters

The hammock swings between apple trees
discarded
disconsolate
your will hangs in the balance.

When winter comes
remember me
for my soul was never at ease
in the snow.

Leave me the birch trees
and the heath smelling of heather
open to sky and winds.

Let me lie down
in fields of lavender
with a backdrop of mountains
and sun flaming to rest.

Murder

It must have been Monday
when Cain brought Yahweh some wheat.
He was pleased with his produce
achieved by the sweat of his brow
just as it should be.
And he was pleased that his brother, too,
had an offering,
his brother Abel so like the lamb
he held in his arms.

Yahweh gazed on them both,
smiling at the younger,
his hair bright in the sun,
and he took the lamb with a gracious nod.

Cain pale with distress
pondered on the word 'sin',
not sure of its meaning.
And words which had not been invented
grew up in the soil he had tilled,
nourished by blood and bone.

♪

Tobias

Into what kind of ear
did those lamentations pour?
A blind man's prayer,
a demonic virgin's weeping.

As for the angel,

come from a void of a celestial mind,
unreal
hallucinatory.

And he lay with a murderous bride
in a room perfumed
with rotting fish.

Desert Fathers

In the long silences of night
the legs cease to have feeling,
the brain stagnates
and a voice hoarse with prayer
breaks inwardly.
Cold, ah, how cold these hours –
even hope dies in God's darkness.

Is it demons we wrestle with
or women, gentle-eyed,
white-limbed? Or bread,
our daily bread, new-baked,
warm to the touch, or fruit,
one perfect apple perhaps,
crisp, with juice enough
to trickle down the beard?

Even in poverty and solitude
there's no certainty of eternal life.
Our souls, the only luxury we own,
suspended in anxiety.

The Mothers

She lives in a stinking pit,
ugly or beautiful
according to the eyes who see her.

The root of all evil,
she destroys all she gives birth to,
she is the curse of men
and seemingly her children.

Her wickedness was uncovered by wise men
who wrote warnings in learned books.

She is beyond death,
which complicates matters
since without her body life would cease –
scientists hope to discover other means
of regeneration.

Meanwhile she begs to be rehoused,
her position reassessed.

Having met her personally
I know her to feel lost, confused
and contrite.

Guilt

'Get out into the world,'
she said.
'Walk across the heath,
scorch your eyes with gorse,
so dazzling in the sun,
or linger in bluebell woods
soak up the countryside,
you'll feel better for it.'

And I walked past a bombed bridge,
picked my way through
a rubble of houses,
dodged a sniper in a cedar tree,
never daring to look
for the lost and lame.

Back in the garden,
safe for a while,
I reflected on the fields of rape,
listened to music
sung by the birds
and wondered if, perhaps,
the last cuckoo had indeed
fallen from the sky.

Always in Another Country

Begin a long way off,
always in another country,
where forgotten places
are never brought to light.

Start again from the beginning,
this time in a cafe,
a cup of coffee on the table,
and then a brick crashes through the window.

Or begin in a street
and a truck passes with people standing
staring in front of them.
Where are they going?
No one asks the question
no one dares answer.

Meanwhile trees are in bloom,
the glass swept from the floor,
no truck in sight.
Think no further.

Just start again,
enter the cafe and order coffee.
When are you going to stop crying?

Advice from a Friend

He said:
'Write about your tears,
let them pour out across the page,
maybe relief will come
in the form of a god or goddess,
who in turn will take the form of a butterfly
or a shaft of sunlight.

Rebuild your house
in another name.
Don't let love vanish into an undergrowth.

True. The world is a bleak place,
it always was,
but who can judge the heart,
let alone the mind?
Living well for a short time
is long enough.'

Waiting

They pass by,
some scrawny,
some without hair.
A name is called
and a woman responds,
unsteady, as she walks
between the chairs
to where a nurse waits.

It's overheated here.
Outside in the sun,
leaves fall
yellow and red on parked cars.

A scream rises,
a protest,
but I am silent.
Love is never enough.

Later, we talk of mundane things
and wonder
if it will rain.

♪

Just Because

Just because the horse
lies down,
it doesn't mean it's dead,
even if it appears so.

Just because one's up against the wall
or on the edge of a precipice,
simply wait,
no further need to worry.

So long as one knows
that only the fool
will look in a mirror
and believe what he sees.

In Retrospect

We all swore we'd die with him,
a moment of emotional bravado.
When it came to the crunch
we did nothing
except stand and watch.

The blood and stench were all too human,
as was his utter loneliness,
his seeming doubt.

We are left in a Hell of questions
on an endless track of remorse.

♪

Mary Reflects

The sun was low in the sky
when they sat down to rest.
'Let us be quiet,' he said.
Below in the valley
a landscape of great beauty,
which may have been partly imagined.
Many unspoken thoughts filled the air
but silence held them lovingly.
Time was running out.

Who was there to see
him lay his head against her naked breast?
Perhaps a swallow dipping and diving
towards the night
or a small spider hanging by a thread from her hair,
which brushed his face.

Martha

Someone has to do it,
prepare food,
clean the house,
wash the clothes.
Someone has to make sure the house is warm,
the roof secure,
yet
Mary has chosen the better part.

Choice?
I didn't choose.
It fell into my lap,
a place allotted to me,
a life of service.

They eat and drink and talk.
My head is in a whirl,
so much to remember while they ask me
to mend their socks,
give them plasters for cuts,
balm for bruises,
to find lost spectacles, keys.
No wonder
Mary chose the better part.

Distracted? Yes
but I listen, observe,
snatch at the odd moment for reflection,
the benefits I reap are many.
Just sometimes I wonder
who, at the end, will hold my hand,
for Mary has chosen the better part.

Martha Continues to Sing

Paul? Yes, I knew him.
He was a brilliant man
but I never really trusted him.
His great conversion always puzzled us.
Something seemed lacking in his soul.
And then the way he pushed us all aside,
took over, almost re-creating the Word we loved.
He frowned on Mary with her long hair
and the legends grown around it.
My part he never guessed,
but no one did. That was a secret
hidden in mystical numbers,
danced and lost in the nights of joy
when we were happy.

And Lazarus, who had reached
the other side and further,
tended the vineyard,
silent as the grave.

A Crusader's Story

The ransom demanded
for the husband of Lady Constancia
was sent by a trusted friend.
He travelled almost non-stop – it was urgent –
the precious bundle wrapped in a golden cloth.

As he set out
she had whispered,

'Never lose it. Don't fail me.'
Her voice faded,
but he kissed her hot forehead
with his lips as a pledge,
wondering if she'd survive the fever,
if her wound would heal.

He rode down the hills
in the glory of Springtime,
down to the coast where the sea
swept the sands, where the boats
came and went.

Grimbald de Pauncefort
sat in the tent of Saladin,
his foot tethered by a chain.
Every day Saladin laughed,
'Still waiting?'
'Never fear,' said Grimbald,
'my wife will send what you ask,
but this holy land is a long way from England.'
'Too far!' came the answer.
His white teeth gleamed in the heat.

One morning a horse with its rider
came to the tent, tired, sweating with strain.
From trembling hands Saladin received the ransom.
Gently he unwrapped the gold cloth
then the fine linen, slightly blood-stained,
and there nestling in moss
lay a hand with a delicate wrist.

'A miracle!' Grimbald exclaimed,
'the hand is still perfect,'
and he wept.

'Your wife must be passing fair,'
said Saladin.
'Go back to her, cherish her.'
He undid the chain round his captive's foot,
'Such love is beyond belief.'

♪

A Soldier Lost to the Regiment

No one will find me here,
here in the native quarter, out of bounds to troops,
with narrow streets
weaving in and out, up and down.

The heat is excessive,
dust flying up with every passing cart,
with the steady tramp of humanity.
My kilt cast aside,
also the woollen socks and heavy boots.
I've kept my trumpet.

Deserter? Yes, from everything but music.
Even my poor mother left to grieve.
I have lost track of time,
all that matters is that I have found the place,
the life, my life, which has been awaiting my arrival.

One day, perhaps,
a distant relative may say:
'I wonder what happened to Fred?
You know, the uncle who went native in India?'

Unlearnt Lesson

Who taught us to pray without ceasing?
God and his angels cannot cope anymore with the prayers
rising so pitifully from the human heart.

Sometimes, God transforms the prayers into clouds,
grey, pink, or black, accordingly.
Sometimes these clouds become top-heavy
and the tears burst forth,
helping to fertilise the soil –
or flood – accordingly.

Only Moses was allowed to see God pass by.
From a cleft in a rock he felt merely
the warmth from a hand, with this he understood
tenderness and compassion.
It took place a long time ago and was lost.
Now, the angels cover their ears
because the wailing, the pleading is unbearable.

Yet we cling to the words that offer hope:
we hope our prayers will be heard
as the mountains shake
the cities fall,
as thousands lie dismembered on battlefields,
in wars taught us by
the bread of suffering,
the water of distress.

Probing Space

Yahweh enjoyed the Big Bang.
'That will keep them guessing,'
he said.
And vanished into a black hole.

♪

The Creator

Further
deeper
into nothingness
within a flower
a bud
within a bud
a flower
reduce all things
to a grain of dust
within the grain
is still no end.
Seek
and you will find
more.

That last great cry
is on all our lips.

Destiny

No one will disturb your dreams,
no one will pluck you from the limousine
gliding towards open country
through a route of trees,
graceful in their massiveness.

Light and dark are all one,
the winds gasp for breath,
and rain stops beating.

No anger, no grief,
just a fusing of mind with forget-me-nots
asleep in a sea of blue.

Saint Francis on the Mountain

Rapt, he sat with the unspeakable name.
Still as death was his third eye.
To ask why the words came too late
is beside the point.

The more he felt, the clearer he saw
how the world became a whirling fire
and the pain of detachment a union
with what had always been.

Two Figures and a Baby

They stood round the village pond,
the baby suspended in the air by an invisible harness.
Silhouettes draped in black,
they spoke of the taste of days,
colour of hours,
smell of dreams.
And they spoke of water,
of nightingales,
the mark of revelation
and when the four horsemen would appear on the horizon.

Their voices raised,
they ignored laughter from onlookers.
All day they stood, patiently,
without moving.
Night came and spectators drifted home, unconvinced,
as the silhouettes became shadows
and the shadows merged in trees.

The words died out
but a baby crying echoed across the valley.
A chill wind moaned in chimneys
and over the pond.

The Chariot

We were walking across the heath,
the sun bright on purple and yellow,
his cloak brushed the heather
as he spoke of things to come
and of what was past.
There was no reason to leave him.
'Today will be the day,' he said.

And then in the distance a cloud
shimmering on the horizon.
The larks fell silent
as a stranger music shook the ground,
and the cloud coming nearer
shaped as a chariot drawn by winged horses.
Their fire swept between us
parting us for ever.

At that moment when my bowels cringed with fear –
no, awe – the sign I'd prayed for,
without knowing why, was upon me,
searing through my fragile shadow,
this nameless identity,
organs, germs, microbes, atoms,
part of a universe still full of mystery.
There was no companion, had never been.
I was alone between sea and heather,
holding a cloak of darkness in hands
which seemed suddenly alien.

For a Friend Abroad

And at that moment
in a field full of snow
looking at the horses
standing so patient behind the fence

loneliness came over you,
came to remind you what it means
to stand patient and waiting
for what may or may not happen.

♪

Suicide

Under a railway bridge
on a cold sunny day
you were pleased to see me.
Fate, you said, our paths
keep crossing.

We walked as far
as the corner,
philosophising.
You told me about yet another
pretty girl,
kissed her,
surprised her,
laughing,
your teeth never fitted.

Did you conserve your energy
all those years,
so you could lie still
at your post mortem?

♪

Night Song

A crow flaps across
the roofs.
All the chimneys are different heights,
different shapes.
The sky is heavy,
there will be a storm.

In the house opposite
is a window-box filled
with half-dead geraniums.
A woman in blue slippers
walks her dog along the path.

Mixed with soot is the smell
of twenty suppers,
none of them exciting.
Washing still hangs by the fire-escape
over at the mansion flats.

The train at platform four
is leaving for Orpington.
More people are coming home,
the walls are moving imperceptibly nearer.

Make-Believe

She'd by-passed
the seven pillars of wisdom,
climbed the steps canopied with
bougainvillaea and honeysuckle.
She was almost breathless
in the scent of attar of roses.
A tinkle of water soothed her ears,
trees long forgotten shaded the path.
This was one of the seven wonders,
a garden, hanging precarious,
zigzag on man-made terraces
overlooking the fairytale Babylon.

Her feet were indeed nimble and light
but she'd not used candlelight
and miles meant nothing.
Wonder she knew about.
The beauty, the mystery all around her
she marvelled and accepted without question.
Wisdom she had none. And the world?
She rinsed her hands in a passing stream.
The world could wait.

Far away was that place.
Long ago the child
who travelled searched
and sometimes found.

Still Learning

In her eighty-third year my sister said:
'It's harder to die than to be born,
I'm just telling you this for your own benefit.'
I've been dying for five years now,
and still wake every morning.

My sister lights another cigarette,
pours herself a glass of wine:
'It makes you sick to hear the doctors talk.'

A Missing Link

All his life he did as he was told.

When his wife died,
he wandered up and down the house
crying: 'Nellie! Where are you?
Ah Nellie! Why did you do it?'

The Sale of Mr Buzby's House

'He never wanted to leave,'
she said.
'He sat on the lawn
and shouted
when they took away the furniture.'

She paused
then spoke again:

'We did what we could,
poor Mr Buzby,
having to pay his way
by selling the house.
He loved every brick,
every moss-covered tile.
It broke his heart
to part with his roses.

Mr Buzby
had gingerish hair
and a slight stammer.
Always kept his food
in an icebox.

Yes, we did what we could,
tried to help,
but the place was too big.
How could he cope?
Everything going to rack and ruin,
brambles growing through the walls.

Did I tell you about the piano?
Once, he played me a nocturne,
D flat major, he told me.
I listened as the sun dipped into night
and I wept a little
at the closing bars.
His fingers were so delicate.'

The Widow

In the morning – swimming,
in the afternoon – dancing
or a brisk walk over the common
with an aging dog.

But as night falls and I return to the darkened house
my heart fails me –
switch on the lamp,
draw the curtains across my life.
I am marking time,
mentally scratch out each day
and yes, always a smile on my lips,
always a joke. Neighbours say:
'How well she copes with bereavement!'
No one knows of hours
alone by the television,
an ache down to the pit of my stomach,
dread of that ice of silence
as I go up to bed.
Sometimes I sit,
not daring to leave the last glimmer
of firelight
or my companion with his paws
comforting my feet.

Life after death?
Let them prove it!
All I can see and expect is
death after life.
Repeat, I am marking time,
filling the hours

with meaningless actions,
not even hoping for the inevitable.

♪

Atalanta

For Susan Hicklin

Hippomenes dropped the grapefruit
as she was passing.
Picked that morning from his own tree,
cared for by Aphrodite,
who whispered to him that hidden in those bushy leaves
was his victory.

To a princess with long limbs for a fortune
love meant nothing.
Always scornful,
her feet carried her over her life,
almost too swift for comfort.

And then
there in her path lay the golden fruit,
a fruit unheard of on that windy coast.
She paused,
stooped, took it in her hand
and sniffed its bitter scent.

He overtook her,
frightened that this trial of strength
would prove his death.
The pounding of his heart blocked out all sound.

Destiny won of course.

Atalanta blamed her father for the defeat,
bear's milk and raw meat
could not compete with grapefruit.

Reluctant, she entered that lush garden,
tamed her wild feet
and learnt to leave an offering to the gods
each day under the mulberry tree –
a cup of wine,
a bunch of grapes
or a bowl of sweet herbs.

♪

Bird Talk

Blackbirds hang about the kitchen door
to remind me they need more food.
Blue-tits and great-tits show their displeasure
by hiding until I refill their feeder.
The robin comes closer and chirps at me:
'Bread will do if there's nothing else.'

As a reward for my help they all gather
near the window, singing and trilling
while I practise a Chopin impromptu.
Come the Spring a blue-tit flies in
looking for a place above the piano
where she can build her nest. Reluctant to leave,
she is back the next day, unafraid of our cat
who is ready to pounce and flashes emerald lights.
I coax the operatic visitor out to the garden,
pause to admire a tree creeper skimming the pear tree.
A wren, perched on the buddleia, is very inquisitive:

loudly she asks where I'm going.
But I have no answer.

♪

Who Can Follow with the Eyes of Sense?

In a mirror I saw the earth,
witnessed wars, famine, cruelty.
I knew no place existed there.
In doubt and anger I denied your presence
finding solace in the birds,
the solidity of trees.
My body shared the changing seasons,
took part in birth and death,
the shedding of leaves.
The world as it goes its way
rends us with feverish longings.
I yearned for knowledge,
sought a meaning of this vale of tears.

But doggedly you followed me,
refusing all denial. At every step
you waited, patient and unyielding.
Then you touched my hand
and I burned for your peace.

So I stand in the cold sunlight
of a winter's morning,
confused by human argument,
frightened by the transience of our days.

Eternity stretches out a hand.
You push me towards it
hiding a smile in the falling snow.

Wartime Incident

In her nightgown,
the child stood between
her fighting parents
and a distraught sister.
As usual her father was drunk,
her mother angry,
and her sister, on leave from the Navy,
was packing a case,
crying and saying over and over:
'I can't stand anymore.'

Outside, beyond the blacked-out windows,
bombs fell,
ack-ack guns boomed,
the houses shook, glass rattled and shattered.

The child, wringing her hands with distress,
ran from parents to sister pleading:
'Oh, please stop fighting!
Please don't leave me alone with them!'

And she was thinking:
How can these people be so stupid,
there's an air raid going on.
We could all be killed.

Paganini Explains

The devil himself admired me.
Bound by one string I improvised magnificently
on my oath of allegiance, right up to my last hours.
I confess those hours were hellishly painful.
My soul, which belongs to no one else,
was violin-shaped from birth.

♪

Thoughts

The church was suddenly full of people,
a noisy bunch,
none of them villagers.
In such confusion
the priest fell silent
and then a brass band pounding triumphant
on the village green.

These strangers,
men, women,
some old, some young,
seemed to belong to me –
wherever I went they would be there.

Running, I made for home
up on the heath,
through the fields,
pushing aside brambles,
stumbling over the heather,
ignoring the sea so clear and blue
on such a day.

Safe on the doorstep of our house,
out of breath,
I turned to check no one was following.
Thankful for peace at last
I opened the door –
and heard footsteps on the stairs.

♪

The Road

Who was he?
Standing there in the sun,
wearing a black cloak
more suitable for Winter than the Spring.
A private investigator?
An actor?
Some would think him handsome.

I met him in the market square,
he raised his eyebrows
and made me shudder.
I took to the road
and now I pause
from sleep to sleep,
to dream
of spices, silks
and that heavy heat
not known in my northern country
where east winds lash the coast.

There's no escape.
There he is,
his cloak flowing out across the dust.

He's smiling,
almost friendly.

He says:
'No need to walk further.
This is our meeting place.'

♪

March 10th

This morning large snowflakes falling
with the rain,
the garden sodden
but birds began their song quite early.

It was quiet in the town,
the florist glad to sell a bunch of daffodils.
We spoke of the cold and our yearning for Spring.

Back at home
the sun shone for a minute
and a glimpse of blue through the window.

A strange birthday celebration,
putting flowers in an empty room.

♪

In Mourning

Not a parting, more a cutting off.
We had said everything there was to say.
Any regret is on my side only.

Your room smells of flowers, not death.
The cat goes in to look for you,
questions your absence with her eyes.
Not a tragedy, just a sadness.
Words come, then peter out.
You yearned to be perfect,
scorned the flesh – which might have made you whole.

Now the quiet of loss echoes round the house.
March winds and daffodils,
a month for birth and a month for dying.

In Memoriam

Rosalie de Méric (1916-1999)

And now let the spirit free.
Let it drift from the house,
from the weight of possessions
and clutter of worries.

Even the branches of trees
hold out a welcome.

Out of dust and dried bone
another form,
recognised only in memory,
as we walk back to familiar places
under the breath of eternity.

For Max

January 3rd 2002

Four o'clock, the light almost gone,
trees black against a fiery sun,
a pheasant disturbs the silence
as he stalks across the lawn.

In my hand one of your cigarettes
from a packet you'll not be needing now.
My heart has been heavy ever since
that summer afternoon when you said goodbye
and somehow I knew we'd not meet again.

It was miraculous
how snow and ice melted last night,
enabling us to sit in the Norman church
and wonder at your violent passing.

And as we stood shivering round your grave,
a robin suddenly lit by the flowers
eyed us cheerfully,
left us with his crumbs of comfort.

♪

The Wake

My hair
floats to the surface.
Terrified
you look away,
stifling a scream.

I see you
through the glass
distorted,
your face like mine.

Neither of us speak.
You try
but
no sound.

Sleep?
Not for me,
nor you,
although you pray.

Love
cut clean,
leaving
a void.

Condemned,
immovable,
I watch,
you wait.

Listen!
Whose heart,
whose heart
do you hear
beating?

Heron

I am filled with longing for the water,
a passion for the sea,
but I am no seagull crying over the beach
or perching on boats in holiday towns,
not the beautiful, vicious creature
that young girls dream about.

No, sad and melancholy, I glide above the marshes,
across the rivers and with phenomenal eyes
search the depths of water
for fish or frogs.
On a winter morning I stand by a garden pond
immobile, intent for the slightest movement
of unwary carp, and the woman of the house
stands amazed at the grace and boldness of my presence.

And though I could tell you tales
which would rival the Arabian Nights –
for I have witnessed and heard strange things
when waiting patiently, half hidden in nettles
or reeds, by an out-of-the-way stream –
my nature is solitary and quiet.
Read what you can of my secrets
in my long-winged flight across your path.

One Evening

For Ron Winkler

Those white pigeons
were dreams
escaping from her heart
and the poet caught them, breathed on them
and they came alive.

He was ready to walk through open doors
and in his eyes she saw
immeasurable heights and depths.

Because of the pigeons
a song transformed
that darkness, which had for seconds
threatened to end all miracles.

Angels

For Herbert Lomas

They appear at the right moment.
Very human in form, quite ordinary,
often someone familiar.
They might arrive at the door
in pouring rain:
'Just dropped in for a chat.'
Or perhaps a chance encounter in the street.
Only afterwards a smile or a word
suddenly becomes illuminated.

Take notice of a silence, a pause
in all the clamour.
Pick up a feather from the ground
and cherish it.

♪

List for the Gardener

For Mary Anne

There's an ancient apple tree to be felled,
Rugosa roses dug out and replanted in the hedge,
overhanging branches of the cherry tree to be cut back.

This is a list for the gardener who never comes.
We wait every week wondering if he will appear.
Is he still young, fair haired and strong?
Or old, gnarled with grey locks tangled in a beard?
Too old, perhaps, to wield an axe or use a spade,
but he could lean on the gate and tell us tales
of village life so many years ago.

In any case it's Winter now, the ground frozen hard,
snow falling. No gardener could be expected on such a day.
We must wait for Spring, avoid the overhanging branches,
forget any gaps in the hedge.
We'll make a new list to leave on the kitchen table.
Then someone will find it and say:
Is this the beginning of a new poem?

The Last Signpost

And when life's sweet fable ends,
Soul and body part like friends;
No quarrels, murmurs, no delay;
A kiss, a sigh, and so away.
                – RICHARD CRASHAW, *Temperance*

At the next signpost
we go our separate ways.
I shall miss you, you know,
we've had good times on the road
but now our time has come to part.
I've taught you a thing or two,
like how to count the stars
and accept with gratitude a bed of moss.

Oh yes, we've sometimes quarrelled –
when I prevented you from squandering
what little money we had left
and worse, when you prevented me
from writing poems to the gods.

Let's remember
the moments we've been close –
the baby, asleep in a magic garden
where forget-me-nots crowded the banks of a stream,
she had a daisy chain around her head –
it was then we became companions
and I thank you for it with all my heart.

Goodbyes are sorrowful
but let me embrace you.
I doubt we'll ever meet again.

Which of our paths are hardest now, I wonder?
You are nearer to the journey's end
but mine is an uphill struggle
and the night is moonless.

♪

Dear Heart How Like You This?

Not much if you must know.
Freely I admit it was self-love
which made me run into your bed,
the mirror having told me
that my hair and white arms
aroused your passion.

It was hardly love
on your part, either,
your eyes already glancing
in another direction.

Romance died later –
or was it earlier?

Scenes from St John's Gospel

Chance Meeting at Noon

It happened when the woman put down her water jar
and he asked for a drink

She knew the word 'prophet' was wrong
they seemed to talk at cross purposes

She teased him at first
knowing all about water
fresh or stagnant
dead or alive

He laughed at her five husbands
her lover

No one recorded what else he told her

But as if from sleep
she saw the fig tree by the well
each leaf quivering with life,
the man, his eyes beams of light,
his voice calling her out of dreams

As though in the silence of her heart
she heard birds sing for the first time
and felt her feet on a path
that would never end

Man without Guile

He never cared for figs
but the tree gave shade,
he sat there. Alone.
Pondering on what is good.

Odd that his eyes were still closed.

In Flagrante Delicto

Much is left to the imagination.
Scent of lavender drifting through the window,
air clean.

A contrast to the town square –
which smells of animal –
where she'd been dragged,
now stood there
wondering what the man –
with dirty feet –
was writing in the sandy soil,
wondering if death was nearer than she'd thought.

And then silence.
The two of them suddenly alone
sun very hot for the time of day.

At last he'd spoken
perhaps smiled
and she remembered the lavender.

Sentenced

Wine turned to blood
in a courtyard
where truth hangs in the air
as hands immersed in water
wash away a life

Noli Me Tangere

She loved him from a long way off,
miles of cloud,
oceans of waves separated them.
Wind chilled her pain.

Not easy trying to live inside his head –
or he in hers –
dividing the unreal from the real.

It was in the garden
where the scent from damp earth
and new-washed flowers
cleansed her mind
that the tips of her fingers
were allowed almost to touch his.

On Patmos

In the beginning
silence
her hands cold
she would stroke my face
and murmur thanks.

We share peace
on this island.
My memories, visions
written down.
Work assigned to me
when Peter asked:
'And what of him?'

My mother of the Word
sits at the centre of the universe
slowly dying into her own thoughts.

Slight Variation on an Armenian Folk Tale

Raphael polished the apples
Gabriel sweetly sighed over them
and Michael aiming with precision
sent them to earth.

The story teller caught them,
he was always a dreamer,
and three apples falling from heaven
set his imagination on fire,
his head so full of words
there left little space for answers.

The listener held one to his ear
heard the pips rattle
and was content.

The wise man ate his apple
he knew and understood what it was for
and
he was hungry.

Puzzling

Here is ME
and there is YOU
but you are also ME.

Both of us began as ME
and certainly will end as ME.

No one in the world is as important as ME,
Africa, America, China, Russia,
hungry, well-fed,
white, pink, blue or black
all ME.

When ME is not looking
YOU are not.
When YOU are not looking
ME is not.

So here is ME
spinning on a globe
aware of the air
and alive like the sheep
in the field
who are probably also ME.

A Monk Converted

He strode through the heat
over scented lotus flowers
crushed them in displeasure
hating their delicate seductiveness

Even in the confessional
mosquitoes plagued his mind
although his body welcomed their sting

How could he confess
his love of water buffalo
his infatuation with tropical life?

Instead he had tried to force the door
desperate to hear those luminous voices
which blotted out the call of monkeys
and orang-utans

Always yearning
half starved for meat and the pulse
of a hunt
his vocation was his great love
for this wild place
which engulfed his spirit

For him God was an immensity
not to be confined under a black robe
in a white-washed cell

For Elizabeth

The lilies sent on the day of your funeral
I left on the table by the window
in case you were around to smell their sweetness

In your hurry to escape
there was no time to admire the plum blossom
very early for the time of year
but amazing in the snow

The Reluctant Prophet

He went back to the womb,
safe from the fierce demands
of a voice which frightened him.
After all, he argued,
I'm not a prophet
and have no wish to be.

Curled snug
head to toe
he dreamt of other worlds,
of people from past lives.

He visualised mountains,
forests, vast plains,
then wrapped his head in seaweed
so he could dream once more
of mermaids swimming in coral reefs.

All the wonders of creation
came to his mind
and he began to sing
a song of praise.

The voice called again
and again,
louder, louder.
Up, up, your return is ordained,
rise to the shore
for the dry land of your life
waits to receive you
and the stones of the city
will tumble at your approach.

Winter Light

It wasn't right for a unicorn
to be out in the rain.
The lady stood by the window watching,
she moved to the door intent on coaxing
the fabulous animal to sit by the fire,
but her brocade skirt hampered her desire.

Summer had passed –
quickly, not without sorrow.
The tapestry in her room
depicted warfare, cruelty
and had taken hours of work
to achieve an exact image.
Too late, she regretted that love was left out.

Removing her skirt, always cumbersome
she also took off her bodice,
with threads of silk
she drew the unicorn into her picture
tethered him fast to an oak's heart.

The lady stood by the window
watching leaves fall into winter
until the trees became as naked as she was.

St Clare

She soothed his burning eyes
bathed blood from his wounds
never commented.

Together
they listened to the sounds
of changing seasons,
learnt to interpret bird song,
wolf's howl.

The miracles which may have happened
and the sacrifice of love
came under her vow of silence,
because once,
she had gathered wild roses in the snow.

Tea Time

My friend's father sat by the fire
reading.
Her mother sat with us
pouring tea.
Bread and butter before cake
always.

And then he was on his feet
shouting,
hands pressed to his head.
What had he remembered
as the children bit into their raspberry slices?

Over and over again
he saw his companions
lying in mud, legs torn off,
faces missing
and above the agony of shells and gunfire
screaming.

I was five years old
knew nothing about war.
Thanked them for having me
and wondered if
I'd been naughty.

Instead of a Letter

Autumn takes over
each day a few more leaves drop
the air has a cooler feel.
Sunflowers turn their heads, and ours,
proud before they fall.

It is time to let go
to accept what comes
if not with joy then just good grace will do.

But coal has to be lugged
food prepared
for the sake of the phenomenon called life.

If only I could send you comfort
in a nearly wrapped parcel
it would smell of red-currants, herbs, roses
and perhaps remind you
that love continues into winter and beyond.

Tell us a Story
to While away the Time

Tell us a story
leave out the nasty bits –
the storm which broke
some years ago
which rages nearer –

Tell us of a country house
shut off from the world
by giant cedars,
there are four children
shut off from the world
by parents' social obligations.

Climb the stairs,
a carpet rather worn
down a hushed corridor
to the nursery.
Here Goldilocks' hair
was brushed till it shone,
here her brothers learnt
to be little gentlemen.

A safe room
with dolls' house,
rocking horse,
the table speaking of honey.

Tell us of glittering crystal
Meissen china
Christmas trees and log fires and
The First Dance.

How Goldilocks married,
all muslin, lilies ...
how her brothers went ...
no, leave out that bit ...

End the story
with a smooth green lawn
sun shining on camellias
and the storm retreating
in the manner of an orderly army.

Sanctuary

He had fled from her –
a wounded animal –
fled to this sanctuary,
his place of worship:
the tree pillars of intricate design,
he knew them all, every branch, twig, leaf, old friends.

From here no glimpse of the castle
where his most hated, most beloved
hid her secret longings behind silk curtains.

No word
no sight of her
for many years.

When war broke out
he fought like other men,
saw death in its various horrors,
felt its breath in his ear
and yet he lived,
returned to his wild cathedral,
safe among the wary animals.

Pain was best endured alone,
to describe suffering
a waste of time.
Love was what really mattered,
without it death was preferable.

And yet he lived
so close to her
that he could read her thoughts.

Each Soul Brings its Own Heaven

For William

That land beyond death
is not so easy to find, my friend.
It's a land which draws the adventurous,
fills them with dread and longing.
A land with houses all awry
dark streets leading to emptiness.

Old loves, familiar things
do not come here.
Those who visit bring back no photographs.

But you must journey on further
into a forest with trees larger than life,
the sun dazzling in Spring,
a mass of bluebells underfoot.

At last, as you embrace the light
the dream of years will wake you
to an ancient knowledge
in a fountain of stars.

Interview with a Displaced Person

What is most memorable?
Perhaps the collar-doves
their sweet voices waking me in the morning.

My father up and about
shouting orders as the servants
hurried to light the fire
hurried to bring him water.

The sound of the pump in the yard
hens squawking, patter of feet,
a new day begun.

And the sun —
the wonderful sun on those special mornings
without a cloud, only a haze of warmth
across the fields
enveloping the trees.

You must understand
that I prefer my childhood to be
just such a summer haze
with a moment or two cut out, as it were,
sharply defined.

Fear broke the dream
fear drove me stumbling over that ploughed land
searching for the railway station
and a hope to find my loved ones
who said we'd meet on the train.

No I never found them.
I survived as you see,
sitting with you
talking of my life
pretending nothing much happened.

♪

Space Travel

Just leave it
no need for luggage
equipment
lie on the bed
and with eyes shut
keep rising up into the welcome universe

Thoughts are tacit
and breath is all darkness

Only the individual traveller
is able to describe the scenery
this is not an ordinary voyage

To return is even quieter
no wasted energy
just a flicker of an eyelid

2 a.m.

Things grow at night
shapes change
and there is always that area
which floats –
it leaves a lump of clay
unshakeable
only a curved moon can shift it.

Words come from the heaving sea
clear, blaze as a furnace in the dark
and shadows move – fleeting, tentative.

If memory is left
it is emptiness
the wind howling vengeance.

♪

Celebration in May

A wedding of a lifetime
a wedding to remember.
All brides want that.

Even those who lie face down
their foreheads touching stone.
Even warm champagne, slightly reddened
by blood from torn skin, is welcome.

Let there be orange blossom, confetti, bullets in the air
and the sun will dry the tears of departing guests.

End of Book

While we're waiting
let's open the champagne
and remember summer is not over yet

This time of evening
makes me sad
and I long for home

How still it is
but the fisherman's wife
said the sea was 'choppy' out there from the shore

Let's not waste these last hours
talking of our past
or speculating on imaginary futures

We're together, I hear your breath,
hold me close
leave the final sentence to the earth